Advance praise for *Table of Plenty*

This book is a uniquely delightful reading experience. It is a captivating integration of narrative about the preparation of delicious food in an Italian family setting, fond sharing of the legacy of a very wise mother, and reflection on the divine call to embrace the goodness, beauty, and truth disclosed within the very deliberate, human experience of intentionally gracious living. *Table of Plenty* is one of those books that a reader will return to again and again—and not just for the recipes, which are wonderful in themselves!

—Ms. Mary Kay Lacke, retired dean of evangelization,
Franciscan University, Steubenville

Dr. Muto has written a compelling book about the intimate connection between the food we eat and the nourishment required for a healthy spiritual life. Those caught up in the busyness of life may know in some way that skipping meals or settling for "quick fixes" are poor choices... *Table of Plenty* shows us what we are missing. Susan tells us "the aim is...to take readers on a journey of faith where food is an entryway to holistic and holy living." In delightful fashion she accomplishes this and more while sharing sumptuous recipes of her mother, Helen, that are time tested in nurturing one's body and spirit, and lead to transforming the heart. I highly recommend this book.

—Fr. Ralph Tajak, O.S.B.,
chaplain of the Epiphany Association

One cannot read this book without finding your mouth beginning to water, or smelling garlic and basil. I found myself in the midst of a warm kitchen amidst Mason jars, fresh spinach, and eggplant, learning to appreciate anew the spiritual importance of the color green and brown, and contrasts in cooking…sweet and sour, hard and soft. I will definitely try some of the recipes and recommend both the book and recipes to others.

—Sr. Sharon Richardt, D.C., PH.D.,
Mater Dei Retreat and Spirituality Center

This book offers wonderfully beautiful perceptions of the dance of spirituality and vitality—an integration of story, recipe, memoir, and inspiration. Its holistic approach to the joy of cooking and the communion of table is an invitation to the finest kind of dining. As a busy mother of five, I very much appreciate the variety of recipes. In owning this book, we have much to enjoy, anticipate, experience, and savor.

—Lori Mitchell McMahon, pastoral associate,
St. Anne Parish, Castle Shannon, Pennsylvania

Table of Plenty

Good Food
for
Body and Spirit

• • •

Stories, Reflections, Recipes

• • •

SUSAN MUTO

Franciscan
MEDIA
Cincinnati, Ohio

Cover design by Kathleen Lynch, Black Kat Design
Cover image © Jill Ferry | Getty Images
Book design by Mark Sullivan

Excerpts from *George Herbert: The Country Parson, The Temple*, edited and Introduction by John N. Wall, Jr. Copyright ©1981 by The Missionary Society of St. Paul the Apostle in the State of New York. Paulist Press, Inc., New York/Mahwah, NJ. Reprinted by permission of Paulist Press, Inc. www.paulistpress.com. Scripture passages have been taken from *New Revised Standard Version Bible*, copyright ©1989 by the Division of Christian Education of the National Council of the Churches of Christ in the U.S.A., and used by permission. All rights reserved.

Library of Congress Cataloging-in-Publication Data
Muto, Susan, 1942-
Table of plenty : good food for body and spirit stories, reflections, recipes / Susan Muto.
pages cm
Summary: "Table of Plenty invites readers into experiencing meals as a sacred time. Author Susan Muto grew up in an Italian family, with a stay-at-home mother whose love for cooking permeates this book. Her prose is highly descriptive and evocative; one feels as if one is right there in the kitchen with Muto and her mother as they go about preparing a meal. Rich marinara sauce, zesty eggplant, a simple loaf of bread and a spinach salad: each becomes an opportunity for reflection on experiencing the goodness of God through the food we eat and the company we share"— Provided by publisher.
Includes bibliographical references and index.
ISBN 978-1-61636-687-2 (paperback : acid-free paper)
1. Food. 2. Dinners and dining. I. Title.
TX355.5.M88 2014
641.5'4—dc23
                                2013041397

ISBN 978-1-61636-687-2

Published by Franciscan Media
28 W. Liberty St.
Cincinnati, OH 45202
www.FranciscanMedia.org

Printed in the United States of America.
Printed on acid-free paper.
14 15 16 17 18 5 4 3 2 1

For my mother, Helen Muto
(1910–1998)
whose death from Alzheimer's disease
assures that her memory
is more alive than ever
in our hearts.

Contents

Preface

Sheer observation of the lives of average Christians may awaken us to the sad fact that spiritual hunger seems to have reached epidemic proportions. Despite the materialistic promises promulgated in the media, you and I know that no amount of power, pleasure, or possession can fill the hole in our hearts. When life's expectations disappoint us, hope may fall off the radar screen like an alien signal that disappears into thin air.

Emptiness of soul despite full stomachs may cause us to retreat to the memory of the good old days. How simple life was then. The information highway had not invaded the calm idyllic days we remember with a nostalgic sigh. Youth never dreamt of rebelling against established institutions. Adults were in charge. Life in general was more agrarian and less automated. In small towns and villages people knew their neighbors. They attended the same schools and churches. They were more in touch with nature. The passing years revolved around the dry and rainy seasons. To retain one's feeling of security was as easy as moving back and forth on a porch swing. In truth, those days had their problems, too, but it's tough to admit that they weren't perfect.

No matter where we are on the road of life in a fast-paced society like our own, we are likely at one time or another to long to sit at a table of plenty with people who appreciate us. As the saint of Calcutta concluded on a visit to America, the disease most prevalent on the streets of any city is loneliness.

A retreat from the present moment to the mythical safety of the past does not diminish our anxiety. While we need to respect the wisdom of what was, we have no choice but to accept with courage what is and will be. The emotional and spiritual stability we crave may not be found until we return to the firm footing of faith. The future is in God's hands, not ours.

Accelerating change may only be a partial cause of our disillusionment. When life moves too fast, we are tempted to ignore the need to reflect on what these changes mean. The journey of faith on which we have embarked in response to God's grace involves risk and conflict, but waters unstirred grow stagnant. Consider the plight of parents sending their children off to school. They worry less about how to fill the empty nest and more about how well these young adults will handle their newfound freedom. Will they remember the rules of moral conduct they were taught? Are the classes and churches they attend, are the safety nets provided by their schools, enough to protect them from irresponsible behavior and outbreaks of violence?

Neither over- nor under-protection can prevent a calamity from occurring. Parents need to pray that their children's decisions will be guided by God. Humility, not arrogance, will enable them to place others' needs before their own and to nourish their spiritual hunger by imbibing the solid food of self-giving love. Otherwise, under the guise of helping others, they may place their own "do-gooding" image first.

The solution to selfishness is not found with the snap of a finger. This gift of charity may only be granted to us if we are willing to change from within and learn from our mistakes. Satisfying vital needs is good and proper but not at the expense of losing our soul.

To monitor the depth or shallowness of our spirituality, we might ask: Are my concerns for others really compassionate or are they rooted in seductive ploys to have the last word? Am I willing to face the consequences of unbalanced living and try to better the lives of those around me? Do I ask forgiveness for the pain I have caused or do I become defensive by refusing to listen to what others have to say? Most of all, do I ask God to detach me from the self-preoccupations that continue to erode my relations with family members and friends entrusted to my care?

Rather than denying our spiritual hunger or rushing to fill it with less satisfactory solutions, we can embrace it as the formation opportunity it is. Do not plants grow stronger when they resist the weeds that choke them? Might not spiritual hunger be God's way of freeing us from the clutches of complacency and readying us for the adventure of faith deepening that awaits us?

In many books and in countless lectures, I have tried to help my readers and listeners to move from linear, informational thinking to formational approaches that allow us to dwell on the texts and teachings placed before us and to savor their meaning. By dwelling on as little as one word or one sentence, as when we slowly chew our food and do not gulp it down, we may begin to change our whole way of being and doing.

Time and again I have seen that just as we are what we eat so we become what and how we read. Spiritual reading is as good for the soul as fine dining is for the body.

Call it my Italian background or my love for cooking, call it my fascination with how food goes from a supermarket shelf to a host's table, call it the thrill of finding a restaurant to which one wants to return and you may have found the reasons why I wrote this book. Keep in mind as I did during the writing process the counsel offered by an Italian saint and spiritual master, Catherine of Genoa (1447–1510), who said, "When I eat or drink, move or stand still, speak or keep silent, sleep or wake, see, hear, or think; whether I am in church, at home, or in the street, in bad health or good, dying or not dying, at every hour and moment of my life I wish all to be in God."[1]

May the sentiments, insights, and skills you find in this book become part of your life as you sit at table, alone and together, not merely to ingest food but also to experience what it means to lead a fuller and richer life at every moment.

Introduction

As much as I would like to cut to the chase and begin this book by revealing the eternal interplay between good food and spiritual growth, there is an unavoidable question I need to ponder: Do bad food and negative attitudes toward eating cause us physical as well as spiritual harm? My reply to this question is an unequivocal yes and here is why.

Food Fears

"The thought of cooking an egg terrifies me." "The moment I enter the kitchen I feel paralyzed." "I've tried to cook, but nothing tastes the way it should." Food fears are familiar to many people eating day after day in restaurants and keeping their refrigerators stocked with bottled water and packaged goods ready to be consumed as soon as the lid is off or the microwave is on. Paradoxically, the more cookbooks one reads or the more food shows one watches on television, the more afraid of preparing a meal from scratch one may become.

Perhaps the best way to grow beyond these always-unfounded fears is to put a stop to projections of failure and let the food, so to speak, prepare itself through you instead of being prepared by you. Too much control tends to mar the simplicity that marks a good meal. Food fears escalate with complexity. The goal is not to become a French chef but to provide simple, solid fare for oneself, one's family, and one's guests. Imagine first who will be eating with you, and set the table accordingly.

Before going to work, set out the placemats, dinner dishes, silverware, napkins, and, if appropriate, wine and water glasses. Add a seasonal touch such as decorative candles. After work, go to the supermarket with three sure-to-please courses in mind. Start with a fresh garden salad made up of ready-to-serve romaine lettuce and baby spinach. Purchase a box of cherry tomatoes, a sweet onion, and a bulb of fresh garlic. Choose for the dressing a ready-made balsamic vinaigrette with extra virgin olive oil. Go to the spice section and get some dried parsley flakes and to the cheese section to purchase a container of shredded Asiago.

Then buy four boneless chicken breasts, two lemons, a box of white sliced mushrooms, and a jar of capers. They should be in the same section where you found the salad dressing. If you don't have these at home, pick up a bottle of extra virgin olive oil, some white all-purpose flour, salt, black pepper, and butter. Get a box of wild rice with cooking directions on it. Then go to the frozen bread case and buy six ready-to-heat-and-eat crusty dinner rolls (while I encourage home-baked bread whenever possible, sometimes you need to rely on bread that's ready to go). Finally, purchase whatever berries are in season, a quart of French vanilla ice cream, and a package of crisp vanilla wafers. If you wish, buy a bottle of white wine like Pinot Grigio or Chardonnay and perhaps a liqueur like limoncella to serve after dessert.

That's the shopping list. It's easy to acquire in about forty minutes with no fear! Remember the food will prepare itself through you and it will be good. Keep it simple. Here's how:

Empty into your salad bowl the bag of chopped romaine and a handful of the spinach leaves for extra color. Wash the tomatoes and add ten of them, cut in half. Peel the onion and chop half of it into the salad bowl along with two diced garlic cloves. Add some salt and pepper and two tablespoons of the dried parsley flakes you purchased. Heat the oven to 425° and bake your dinner rolls for ten minutes as you want to serve them with the salad. Don't forget the butter! Plate the fresh greens and sprinkle them with Asiago cheese. Let your guests add the amount of dressing they like. Serve it on the side—not from the bottle. It looks better that way.

Following the directions on the box, start cooking the wild rice; this will usually take about forty-five minutes to cook.

Next unwrap your four chicken breasts and lightly coat them with flour. In a nonstick pan, heat on medium-high a tablespoon each of butter and olive oil. Cook the chicken for about four minutes on each side. Remove the breasts from the pan, lower the heat, and add to it the juice of one lemon and three teaspoons of capers. Let the mixture come to a slow boil and return the breasts to the pan, turning them a few times until they are juicy. Let them simmer for about ten minutes and top the chicken with a few turns of sea salt and pepper. Then sprinkle the whole delicious mixture with some parsley flakes.

Heat some olive oil and butter in another pan. Add some chopped sweet onion and a garlic clove, and as soon as they start to sizzle add the rest of the spinach to the pan turning it quickly until it reduces itself to a lovely sautéed green (about five minutes, at most) to complement the rice and the chicken. Look at the beautiful dinner plate you've created: lemon-caper chicken, wild rice, sautéed spinach—ready to serve as soon as your guests finish their salad.

While they are relaxing over the last bite and perhaps sipping some more chilled white wine, excuse yourself and go to the kitchen (which may become your new favorite room freed of all food fears!) and scoop some ice cream into a dessert dish. Top it with the fresh berries, and if you'd like, pour over it a spoon of the liqueur you purchased earlier, or which you already have on hand. Serve it with the vanilla wafers to add that extra touch everyone loves. Make coffee if anyone wants a cup. Ask if they need some more water or wine and relish their compliments to the chef.

Food Threats

I wanted to spend time dispelling food fears, but I would still like briefly to identify some other bad food habits. One that readily comes to mind is that of food threats: "Either finish your vegetables or plan on spending the rest of the evening alone in your room." "How dare you push that plate aside when I slaved all day in the kitchen preparing it." "Either you clean your plate or you go hungry. There's no in between!"

Using food as a way to threaten a child or an adult into cringing submission is a sure formula for retarding spiritual growth. Threats have a way of rendering food tasteless anyway. So who wants to eat? Better to starve than to give in to a "food bully."

Food Indifference

A third danger of dividing body and soul is food indifference. "I'll eat anything anyone puts in front of me." "It all tastes the same anyway; it's just there to fill me up." "What's the use of getting excited about how something looks or tastes?"

Perhaps this kind of indifference is inevitable in institutional settings such as hospitals, but it is a guaranteed way to shrink the soul and make life a study in colorless getting up and equally colorless going to bed. There may be another excuse for indifference when one simply does not have enough to eat. To stave off starvation one is willing to consume almost anything. But on a day-to-day basis it is a sad state to foster a climate of careless indifference to the gift of good food and its potential to heighten virtues like appreciation and cordial fellowship around a caring table.

Food indifference harbors distinct dangers. When a person doesn't care about what he or she consumes, the price to be paid is often harm to one's body. What difference does it make if I fill up on junk food? Overeating one day leads to undernourishment the next. The body is on a roller coaster of too many nutrients or not enough. We lose track of the words Paul wrote to the Corinthians: "Do you not know that you are God's temple and that God's Spirit dwells in you? If anyone destroys God's temple, God will destroy that person. For God's temple is holy, and you are that temple" (1 Corinthians 3:16–17).

What is troubling about such a willful defeatist attitude to life is not only a lack of attention to health, along with beauty and order, but a second and related danger of dualism. The body does not count. One can even attribute this careless stance to "holy indifference," misunderstood as rising above matter rather than as exercising prudent detachment from what is in excess.

Be wary of becoming indifferent to what you eat. It can erode the link between body and soul. From a biblical perspective, food is proof of the generosity and providence of God. There is no lack of excess coming from the hand of the Most High. Five thousand are fed from a few loaves and fish and twelve baskets are left over. Not fifty but a hundred and fifty-three fish miraculously weigh down the net of experts who have fished all night. Starting in the Garden of Eden, humans are invited to eat of every seed-bearing tree and to enjoy the life burgeoning from the green, green earth.

In a way the Lord revealed the truth of a slogan I heard often from my mother's lips, "The way to a man's heart is through his stomach." How many were the incidents where the Lord of hosts before and after the incarnation of Jesus offered lessons in evangelization by feeding the people—from manna in the desert to the loaves and fishes? Empty stomachs miraculously filled definitely heighten our attention to the mystery of abundant provision and the pleasure it gives us.

A custom my mother initiated and maintained, especially at festive seasons like Thanksgiving and Christmas, was to add to an already-displayed cornucopia of plenty a surprise dish that went beyond our expectations. We knew we could count on a casserole of succulent sweet potatoes baked with freshly squeezed orange juice and honey to complement the turkey, but what a surprise it was to realize she had taken the time to make her own cranberry jelly and forgo the convenience of opening a can. The food of love once again announced itself without a word. That's what makes one believe that Jesus's appeal to hearts and stomachs was more persuasive than preaching the same doctrinal truths from a remote podium.

Such generous giving merited equally generous distribution in turn. What good would it do for the king to ready a banquet to which no invited guests would come? Nothing pleases a cook more than guests who relish what he or she serves. Compliments to the chef, perhaps complemented in a family setting with a grateful hug, is all the reward she wishes. Does it not stand to reason that the Lord who loves a cheerful giver pours out no less affection on a cheerful receiver?

A wave of shame ought to overtake us when the Lord, who gives himself to us wholly in the Eucharist, offering us the banquet of his own Body and Blood, is received with a yawn. Are there any sadder words in Scripture than these: "He was in the world, and the world came into being through him; yet the world did not know him" (John 1:10)? Sad as well is his lament that he had been with these people for a long time now and still they do not know him (John 14:9).

To be a taker of food or any other commodity without appreciation diminishes our humanity. The height of selfishness corresponds to the avaricious depths of assuming that we are the reason the giver exists. Mother's table is for me; all the thanks she needs is for me to eat my fill of what is on it. She is the cooking machine and I am the consumer of the fuel she provides. Such a mechanistic model of indifference is as dehumanizing for the one who eats it as it is for the one who prepares and serves the meal.

Food freely given exacts from us a promise to go beyond its selfish reception to the unselfish realm of deep gratitude. There we commit ourselves to give to others what we have received. My food mentors— grandmother and mother—cooked not because their sense of dignity depended on others' opinions of them but because they knew that treating tablemates to the best they could offer (even during the Great Depression) was the backbone of every family and nation.

Though ingratitude and indifference might have come to their table, it disappeared when they left it. Poured forth from previously pursed lips was a litany of gratitude complemented by what these good souls always wanted to see: sighs and smiles of contentment. These dear women echoed in their own way these touching words from the prophet Isaiah:

> Ho, everyone who thirsts,
> come to the waters;
> and you that have no money,
> come, buy and eat!
> Come, buy wine and milk
> without money and without price.
> Why do you spend your money for that which is not bread,
> and your labor for that which does not satisfy?

Listen carefully to me, and eat what is good,
and delight yourselves in rich food. (Isaiah 55:1–2)

Chapter One

Heavenly Eats

"Eat to live," my mother often reminded me, "don't live to eat." A woman whose small frame cradled a large heart, she lived what she taught. Mother's innate wisdom prevailed when it came to understanding the spirituality of really good food, capable of nourishing body and soul. Food, its cultivation, preparation, and presentation, finds its way into every religion on the face of the earth. While our appetite for food can be mortified by ascetical practices, fasting must always be done with moderation. Heroic virtue is one thing; erratic heroism, unresponsive to the grace of God and prone to separate body and spirit, is another.

A slight, to say nothing of a severe, waning of our vitality is an instant reminder of our mortality. Without enough to eat and drink, we will die. The emaciated rib cages and bloated bellies of starving people make us all advocates for the cessation of world hunger. No sooner do food banks empty than citizens rush to fill them again, cognizant of the need that there are always hungry people to be fed.

The rights to food, clothing, and shelter are basic to the human condition. We protest the poisoning of our ecological systems; we demand that legislators do not allow greed to despoil our food chain and the natural resources it draws upon. Poets and pundits have long pointed to farmers and ranchers who treasure the land and work to feed the masses as among the best of our citizenry. Urban dwellers want to shop at farm markets and smell the earthy perfume of fresh produce.

Many today seek to eat "whole foods," organically grown meat, fish, vegetables, and poultry, unprocessed grains, and chemical-free beverages. Citing their benefits to the body leads to convincing arguments concerning their positive effects on mind and will. Good and bad moods are directly related to what one consumes. Both cooks and those they serve want to know where their food has been grown and how it got to market. The spread of bacteria in unclean processing plants frightens everyone. Food poisoning is a terrible experience. One who has had it wants to prevent it at all costs. Since we must eat to live, we expect our food to be safe and we insist that those who prepare it do so in squeaky-clean kitchens.

Happily for us, instinct poor though we may be, sheer biology plays a huge role in the eating process. We can smell something cooking "a mile away." How food is plated either appeals to our sense of sight or not. We can touch or smell a melon and tell if it is ripe and ready to eat or if it needs to sit for a time. Potato skins, thinly peeled and deep fried, that crackle in our ears may appeal to our taste buds as much as the touch of cold, crunchy celery dipped in dill sauce. We know when we are hungry because our stomachs growl. We have some awareness of how much to eat and of when to stop because we feel full—although we may not always pay attention to our fullness. We know what tastes good to us and what we cannot stand to eat.

Some of us are allergic to certain foods such as cucumbers (in my case), which others crave. Most know the difference between dining in a fine restaurant and wolfing down an order of fast food. In the best of times, we experience a wedding between the body's need for nourishment and the soul's longing for an experience that fills not only our physical but also our spiritual emptiness. Food for the body ought not to be seen as an end in itself but as a means to nourish the hunger longing to be satisfied in our souls.

A contemporary researcher, Corrie E. Norman, writes of the experience of "savoring the Sacred." She believes we can better understand the religions of the world if we pay attention to the way food is procured, prepared, and eaten by their adherents. The spicy foods loved by traditionally Islamic cultures, the elaborate tea ceremonies conducted by Far Eastern devotees of Zen Buddhism, and the rules governing kosher cooking in certain branches of Judaism are but a few examples of the connections between religion and food.

Food also plays a huge role in our remembrances of childhood. It is the backdrop we use to introduce strangers to new friends. One current dating craze is to meet "just for lunch." Corporate expense accounts support meals with clients and other people important to business connections because conversations that deepen relationships and seal good deals go on long after the table has been cleared.

The language of food is universal. Whether we come to eat in a hut in the wilderness or a household in which a perfectly laid table awaits us, it is a worldwide gesture of hospitality to offer food and drink, whether it is served on a fern leaf or in a petite cup.

Many faith traditions instruct adherents to match the way they eat to what they believe. Some even forbid the consumption of certain foods dubbed unclean or unholy. Other foods take on a deep symbolic significance. Bread, wine, and fish are exemplary Christian foods, so much so that these gifts of human hands become the main evidence of Christ's presence among us. After all, was it not he who took a few loaves and two fish and fed the multitude? After the resurrection, did the disciples not know him as the Christ in the breaking of the bread? Even the bowls from which food is consumed and the utensils one uses can become invested with sacred power. In a home where a saint once lived, items such as cups, saucers, or spoons that touched his or her holy lips may be respected as relics.

Eating is not only an individual delight but also, and mainly, a communal experience. Family reunions mean sharing story after story around the table. The food served becomes the backdrop for a renewal of mutual concerns remembered and new events announced. Those of us who have to travel for business may need to eat alone, but may not relish doing so. Travelers often end up at a local hangout not only to order a beer but to find a bartender or other patrons to converse with. Breaking bread with a friend is why I baked that loaf in the first place. A dinner scheduled to last for perhaps two hours can put us in a zone of leisure that seems to go on without our knowing how so much time has passed.

When I was in Holland in 1996 to celebrate the Golden Jubilee in the priesthood of my friend and colleague, Father Adrian van Kaam, (1920–2007), his special feast began at noon and did not end until final toasts at six o'clock that evening with no sensation of the clock's chime. We were definitely in a *kairos*, not a *chronos*, mode of being.

That day taught me that eating ought to be not merely a consumptive but mainly a contemplative experience. It is not a question of how much or how little we eat. Vitality can wane whether we have not enough or too much food, whether we leave a table still feeling empty or being terribly bloated. When instead we connect our vitality to our spirituality, eating immediately becomes more than a routine act comparable to filling the gas tanks of our cars. It is an event full of meaning. Enjoying really good food—tasty, well-balanced, and prepared with love—is a distinctively human experience. It overrides mere instinctive directives to fill our bellies and draws us into the realm of laughter and light banter, playful and serious discourse. At the highest level, eating can resemble a form of ecstasy, as when a diner surrounded by the sight, smell, touch, taste, and sound of exquisite food says, "I'm in heaven," or, "It doesn't get any better than this," or, "That's perfection on a plate."

Modern life lived at a hectic pace has made us adept at eating on the run. We gulp instant beverages such as coffee and soup prepared in less than a minute. We eat in our cars and at our desks not to lose any time. Fast food gratifies our vitality at the expense of our spirituality. We can't even remember what or when or if we ate! We live to eat, failing to realize that animals do the same. There has to be something more to nourishment than merely filling up an empty cavity.

To ponder the spirituality of really good food suggests that we may have to reawaken the art and discipline of what it means to "taste and savor." Instead of swallowing our food almost whole, we may have to ruminate upon it as we ought to do with a favorite text. When a dish is as delightful to see as it is to eat, it ought not to embarrass us to ask for a second helping. Rather than rushing to leave the table, we may discern that slower eating is as necessary for bodily nourishment as slower reading is for spiritual enlightenment.

Good food, like a good book, has to be ingested and digested if we are to derive its benefits. It harms our digestive system to eat with one hand and to talk on the phone with another. No wonder antacids are pharmaceutical bestsellers! Most of us feel that dining with china, not paper, with knives and forks, not plastic utensils, with time to taste, not rushing though a meal are better for us, body and soul. Finger food has its place, perhaps at a cocktail party, but it is so enriching to sit and dine at a beautifully set table, enjoying pleasant conversation and food prepared with the sole intention of pleasing one's guests.

In the Bible there are at least seven hundred references to eating, not counting those to drinking and sharing food or preparing meals. The *Dictionary of Biblical Imagery* declares with confidence that "eating is a master image of the Bible." It combines literal acts like a wedding feast with figurative events as lofty as working miracles. The physical experience of munching corn yields a spiritual declaration of just who is the Lord of the Sabbath.

For the chosen people, ceremonial laws and rules overseeing how and what people ate pertained to health measures as well as to the revelation of covenant signs of God's love. Providing gifts such as manna in the desert to ward off starvation made the chosen people see the loving providence of their Creator. Having food to eat when we are hungry is a reminder of how dependent we are on earth, sun, sea, and sky, on a mystery of love that embraces and sustains our being.

Our existence at its most elemental dimension depends on food.

Once when we asked my little nephew to lead our family in prayers before our Thanksgiving meal, he said, glancing at his mother: "God is grace. God is good. Thank her for this food. Amen." Eating evokes expressions of gratitude for our survival, but it also signifies the sheer vulnerability of our human condition. Homeless people on any street do not know whence their next meal will come.

Around the world, if crops fail due to flood or drought, whole populations face the horror of starvation. Miracles do occur, as when God commanded ravens to feed the prophet Elijah in the morning and evening (1 Kings 17:4–6) or when the widow's oil jar never ran dry (1 Kings 17:8–16). We can hardly think of Jesus without remembering the times he miraculously fed the crowds who followed him. Not everyone can expect miracles, though, and we should always be mindful of those who do not have enough.

In the West, especially, we have come to expect that our food supply will never run short. So endless is its array that we throw away almost as much as we consume. Whether our food is processed or fresh, we assume there is something for us to eat in the pantry or on the nearest supermarket shelf. Some eat too much and turn their eyes away from the hungry. They complain about obesity and start fad diets while others never have the satisfaction of feeling full.

Christianity is one religion that places upon us the obligation to care for the least of our sisters and brothers here on earth if we want to share the banquet the Lord of hosts has prepared in heaven for those who believe. The image of an overflowing cornucopia reminds us that eating ought to be not only an obligation but a celebration. Such a table is a sign of hospitality. When a cook prepares everything from scratch for her guests, no one doubts the efficacy of her loving care for each ingredient. Everyone leaves the table in a jovial mood, satisfied in body and soul, having been the happy recipients of another's hospitality. We leave the table with a full stomach but, more important, our spirit feels bathed in the warmth of love.

The vital act of eating may seem to be a neutral event, but it has about it both moral and immoral overtones. To feed hungry strangers is as much a moral act as to provide hospitality for familiar guests. To snatch food from the mouths of babes or the frail elderly, to turn a stew into a poisonous brew, to disobey a prohibition meant for our own good, as when our first parents ate of the forbidden fruit or when a greedy restaurateur deliberately serves tainted goods, all these are immoral acts. It is as sinful to become gluttons as it is to fast for wrong reasons, such as showing others how impious they are compared to us.

Eating is not a neutral act. It is a mirror of our lifestyle and an expression of our commitment to be life-givers. By having supper with sinners

(Luke 15:2), Jesus widened the recipients of salvation from the chosen people to all who believe. He invites us to the supper of the Lamb (Revelation 19:9) as the culmination of our having eaten his Body and drunk his Blood in the Eucharistic celebration.

In these few examples from the Bible and our own lives, we have come to see that eating is not only a physical act but also a spiritual event. It affects our bodies and our psyches at the same time. It influences the way people picture themselves as loveable or despicable. In a "thin is better" world, even the most minuscule portion of food on one's plate becomes an enemy to combat. Some of us, surrounded by abundance, die of self-willed starvation. Others, surrounded by want, would "kill" for a crumb dropped from a rich person's plate. Counting calories or having no calories to count spells the difference between wealthy and indigent civilizations. Not in question is the beauty and dignity of everyone's personhood; what concerns us is the value we place on what and how we eat.

Food is a symbol of our gratitude to God and our mutual appreciation for one another. It is a commodity to share as well as an expression of how much we care. Feeding the hungry is a virtue that must never be forgotten, dining with friends a value we cherish all the more. It is good to celebrate those moments—rare as they may be—where companionship around the table becomes a form of communion, where fantastic food seals friendships, where our vitality and our spirituality truly "wine and dine" together.

Food for Thought

God said, "See, I have given you every plant yielding seed that is upon the face of all the earth, and every tree with seed in its fruit; you shall have them for food." (Genesis 1:29)

Plow a furrow, plant a seed, pick an eggplant. How and when did that happen! The fluidity and efficiency of the food chain evokes awe. Start with a seed so tiny it's hard to see. Put it in potting soil. Watch the leaves sprout. Transplant them and voila! A bunch of basil or a plume of parsley. What happens with the help of sun and water seems magical to the naked eye. One day brown dirt, the next a row of green beans.

Might we draw an analogy here to the way grace works? Our hearts feel parched, our spirits like desert dust. Then the rain of grace washes over us and we behold the sun of God's mercy. Like the seed that must go underground and die so that new life may come forth, so we, too, die to our ego-self and rise to the true Christ-self we are.

On days when I feel a bit let down (everyone does once in a while), I turn to my kitchen as if it were a therapy room and tell myself how much better I'll feel when I cook a hot meal and forget my troubles. Life picks up the moment I decide to reproduce to the best of my ability my mother's recipe for Eggplant Parmagiana.

In my refrigerator I have three medium-sized eggplants, which I proceed to peel, slice one-quarter-inch thick, salt generously, and let stand for fifty minutes or so. I rinse the slices in cold water, squeeze them gently to remove the excess, and dust both sides with a dry rub consisting of one cup of flour, a tablespoon of cornstarch, and a seasoning of black pepper, oregano, and paprika. I then beat together a batter of one tablespoon of cornstarch, one-quarter cup of cream, five eggs, salt and pepper, freshly chopped basil and parsley (two table-spoons each), one teaspoon of chives, and two tablespoons of cream sherry.

Now I set on the stovetop a large skillet coated with olive oil. I dip each slice of eggplant in the batter and fry it crispy on each side. The slices must not be overdone. Watch them turn a light golden brown. Lay them on a platter atop paper towels to absorb any excess oil. Add oil to the frying pan as needed. By this time, the blues I felt have flown out the window and creative cooking has performed its therapeutic task.

The next step is to arrange the crispy slices of eggplant in a flat casserole pan alternating them with Italian tomato sauce (the recipe is on page 104) and a generous helping of grated Pecorino-Romano. A taste of Parmesan completes the dish before it goes into a 325° oven to bake and bubble for an hour.

The sauce, which can be made ahead of time and can be used for any pasta marinara dish, requires that I sauté gently in olive oil two cloves of garlic, thinly sliced, one diced sweet onion, one small green pepper, and one small red pepper. Use a deep pot with a lid. Into it pour a quart-sized can of crushed tomatoes, a small can of tomato paste, and a half-cup of vegetable broth. When the sauce comes to a boil, add a quarter-cup of Marsala wine, and two tablespoons each of freshly chopped parsley and basil. Add salt and pepper to taste.

Let the whole mixture simmer for ninety minutes. Use this savory sauce to cover the eggplant before putting it in the oven with another coating of Parmesan cheese and some red pepper flakes to add a little zing! When this flavorful dish is ready, let it sit for about twenty minutes before serving. Toast some garlic bread to accompany it, invite a few friends to share the meal, and open a bottle of red wine such as Pinot Noir to chase the blues away once and for all.

Thoughtful Food

As long as we are on the subject of food as a source of healing, it would behoove us to consider the legendary role played by chicken soup. Whether its power to soothe the symptoms of the common cold is real or not, it would be wise to make a homemade pot the moment symptoms appear. Here's how to do it from a family recipe handed down from my ancestors and embellished to the point, dare I say it, of perfection.

Soulful Soup

First go shopping for the following ingredients, added to whatever you have on hand.

- A fresh, plump roasting chicken, weighing 2 to 2½ pounds
- One 16-ounce box of chicken broth
- 4 chicken bouillon cubes
- 6 carrots, peeled and cubed
- 6 celery stalks, cubed
- 2 medium white baking potatoes, peeled and quartered
- 2 medium-sized sweet potatoes, peeled and halved
- 1 cup sweet onions, quartered
- ¼ cup cream sherry
- Juice of half a fresh lemon
- Handful of freshly chopped parsley
- Salt and pepper to taste, with a pinch of thyme

Here are the steps to follow to make a truly "soulful soup."

Cut the chicken in half, thoroughly wash it, and discard the wrapped parts. Be sure the inside is cleaned thoroughly. Lay the chicken halves in the bottom of a five-quart stainless-steel pot with a lid. Cover the chicken with five to six cups of distilled or filtered water, then add the chicken broth.

Put the pot on medium-high heat and add all the other ingredients. Be sure enough water is in it to cover everything—not too much, not too little! Bring the soup to a boil and then cook it on low heat for at least four hours. When the chicken is cooked thoroughly, take it out and put it in a separate bowl to cool.

Take a colander and put it in a pot large enough to hold the broth and all the vegetables. Strain everything and press it a bit to get out all the juice. Into the strained broth put the carrots, the sweet onion, and the white potatoes only. Discard the rest of the vegetables. Strip from the cooked chicken all the good white and dark meat (no bones and no skin). Add the meat to the broth with the carrots and potatoes. Taste for flavor and add salt and pepper as needed.

Return the soup to a low fire for about two more hours. Let everything simmer slowly.

When ready to serve, boil a cup of Acini de Pepe (pastina) and drain it before adding it to the soup with the chicken pieces and vegetables. Chop fresh parsley to put on top of each serving bowl with a spoon of grated Parmesan or Romano cheese.

Every sense will be alert to this soulful soup, and its healing property takes hold with the first spoonful. Expect requests for more than one bowl.

Chapter Two

Let's Eat

When my mother, Helen Scardamalia Muto, died of Alzheimer's disease on December 21, 1998, I lost not only an eighty-five-year-old friend, but a cooking mentor and dining partner. One of the saddest consequences of AD is the way it deprives its victims of their taste buds and eventually even their memory of good eats. In the end they are hardly able to enjoy anything but the sweet softness of an ice cream treat. It's hard to coax food into a mouth that refuses to chew and a throat that forgets how to swallow.

While this dreadful disease robbed me of my mother's mind and her "human doing," it could not steal her spirit, her essence, her "human being." Neither could it snuff out my memory of the dining pleasures she gave us as a family nor of the delight she took in preparing and serving more fine meals than any of us could count. AD crushed her vitality but not her spirituality. She may have lost her memory of tasty dishes, but we did not. Her recipes are the test kitchen around which our family continues to cook and eat: "Remember Nunny's recipe for chicken soup…adding the juice of half a lemon, freshly squeezed…that was her secret ingredient…everyone asked for second helpings…she would have loved that.…"

My mother benefitted from the lessons she inherited from my maternal grandmother, Elizabeth, whose infectious spirit could not be killed by stomach cancer. What a woman she was! Her faith moved mountains. She did not need perfume; she smelled of freshly baked bread and homemade sausage. My sense of smell is inextricably linked to basil and garlic, fresh herbs such as parsley and thyme that grew in her garden, and plum tomatoes simmering on the stove. The ingredients she added to them resulted in the finest, freshest marinara sauce I ever tasted. She was another woman whose vitality and spirituality were one and the same.

I was the blessed beneficiary of the combined presence of two vivacious women who reverenced good food for God's sake. I think they understood its healing power. No matter what state we were in when we approached their table, we always felt better when we got up. Ours was an experience of not just eating but of being healed and caressed by excellent meals. An invitation to dinner proved to be as nourishing to our bodies as it was to our souls.

The aim of these reflections on eating as a spiritual experience is not to produce a cookbook but to take you on a journey of faith where food is an entryway to holistic and holy living. There ought to be no split between a full stomach and a happy soul. When a dish is wonderfully prepared, thoughtfully presented, and thoroughly enjoyed, it mirrors the dance of life between vitality and spirituality. The head relaxes and the heart expands. Eyes twinkle. Smiles break forth. Conversation ebbs and flows and clock time diminishes to a more leisurely pace.

The best formula for overcoming the heresy of dualism or for splitting mind from matter is to remember when dining that we are not a body one minute and a soul the next. We are enfleshed spirits and spirits in the flesh. By recalling to my mother's everlasting honor the way the food we treasured in our home was then and ought now to be prepared, I hope to show what a powerful force eating is in our spiritual journey from birth to death. We begin life sucking on a nipple or a bottle. We end our days on earth as my mother did, sucking her last ice chip before taking her final breath. In between are those most memorable experiences we can try to recollect—ones in which breaking bread is not only a celebration of our humanness but also a reminder of our communion with the Divine.

Following my mother's death, it was my duty and my joy as her only daughter and eldest child to go through her closets, drawers, and papers to preserve mementos that merited being shared with my two brothers, my sisters-in-law, and her grandchildren. The main treasures I found were not monetary, for Alzheimer's care had claimed those. They were her artworks—a collection of oil paintings, watercolors, and acrylics (she was an artist from the age of fifty-six until five years before she died)—and a shoebox full of handwritten recipes with her notes on how to execute them and what to do to make sure that everything we cooked tasted and looked its best.

The more I read over these scribbled notes, the more familiar I became with her indomitable spirit. My mother wanted people to feel terrific—vitally and spiritually—when they left her table. She appreciated her diners as much as they loved her dinners. In resurrecting her favorite recipes, we were to adhere to only one standard: "Does it taste the way Mother would have made it?"

When stomachs are empty, there is nothing we want more than to feel full. And yet our distinctively human spirit longs for something beyond the mere satisfaction of vital cravings. Whether we know it or not, we want to dwell on a higher plane of meaning from the start to the finish of our meal. No wonder there is nothing worse than food so casually readied and swiftly consumed that we cannot wait to leave the table, almost wishing we had never eaten at all.

Think of the difference between a homemade meal and what it is like to shovel onto one's plate batches of commissary food that tastes as bland as it looks. Notice how many people reach immediately for the salt and pepper shaker or the Tabasco sauce. It would be foolish to deny the difficulty of feeding scores of hungry students in schools or patients in hospitals. It is not my place to critique these noble intentions but to call attention to why food, with the smallest amount of care and creativity, can be as uplifting to consume as it is nourishing to eat.

There is no excuse for severing the tie between spirituality and vitality. There are retreat houses to which people return to be fed spiritually because the food is spectacular. Often, one of the first questions one asks when a friend or relative leaves the hospital is, "How was the food?" Were you in that situation, what would your answer be?

The first scrap I found in mother's recipe box made me smile from ear to ear. My mother was not known for her shyness. She was an extremely outspoken Italian American woman. If someone needed a dose of honesty, they knew to whom to go to find it. She told it like it was and pulled no punches. "There's nothing worse than a phony," was one of her oft-repeated sayings. The first thing I found in her box was not a recipe, but a list titled "Some Thoughts Concerning Foods That Turn Me Off."

Three of them are worth repeating for all would-be cooks. Number one details her thoughts on "How to ruin a perfectly good meal." She writes, "Having too much alcohol or other beverages to drink before eating is the best way to spoil one's dinner; it makes the cook's efforts an exercise in futility." She believed that serving wine at the table complemented the cuisine, "on the condition that one does not overdo it." Keeping everything in moderation, not just alcohol, but spices and portions, was her primary rule. Excess in any form, she held, damages our health; it violates our natural bent toward balance. Gluttony is a cardinal sin for good reason.

The desert tradition, critical to the growth of Christian spirituality, warned disciples to moderate their tendency toward too much fasting and to exercise strict obedience when it came to practices like "taking the discipline." Bending a bow was one thing, breaking it another. One disciple was so proud of his ascetical practices that his spiritual father advised him to go out and get a good temptation that he might be worth something in the reign of God. In his famous Rule, St. Benedict of Nursia prescribed a community life based upon mutual support, obedience, hospitality, tolerance, and moderation.[2]

Mother's second caution concerned "so-called appetizers" that could spoil a meal as much, if not more so, than too many before-dinner drinks. Chips, creamy dips, crackers with strange droppings on them, cheap cheese bits, pickled this and that, and other finger-licking nibbles were subject in her book to total dismissal. Why would anyone want to fill up on junk food when a banquet was about to be served? She was not opposed to appetizers on one condition: that they were as fresh and delicious as dinner itself and a perfect complement to the menu.

Mother's observation led me to a brief meditation on the eternal banquet that awaits us in heaven. How can we expect to feel hungry for the Holy in eternity if we settle while on earth for the junk food of self-indulgence? Are we so busy gratifying our whims that we miss the many graces and blessings God invites us to enjoy? Does the "me" that slips into the center of our lives cancel our attraction to the "mystery"?

The problem goes beyond bad eating habits. It's about wanting more of what never lasts as if it were ultimate. In truth, we ought to focus less on what gratifies us and more on what makes others grateful for us. Americans have a reputation for being fast food addicts. We gorge on almost anything. Only recently have we begun to read the labels on the goods we buy.

Not everything we crave belongs in our stomachs. It's a sensitive organ, deserving of tender loving care. Mother's single rule to keep our weight at a healthy level works as well as any about which I've read: Never eat in between meals and don't fill up before you start to dine. "Don't forget," she said with certitude, "less is always better than more." I believe she meant, "Edit your food copy before you fill your plate, eat the right portions, fresh not processed, and you won't have to worry about gaining weight."

Her third beef had to do with bad-mannered people who show up too early for dinner and leave too late! What this counsel taught me was that sitting around the dinner table can evoke a whole constellation of virtues and vices. Mother's first intention toward any guest who walked through the door was to make him or her feel at home. She knew that hospitality was healing. Hungry people are not that different from hospital patients. They need tender loving care. Comfort food is important. That chicken soup mentioned in the previous chapter was medicine. I feel certain it made us well when we were sick with colds, flus, and fevers.

Guests with good manners also understand that timing a meal is as challenging as preparing it. To appear too early can place the host or hostess under terrible stress. He or she may not have had a chance to finish the meal, or to change out of clothes that may be covered with the evidence of food preparations. To be late can cause moist dishes to dry up, placing a burden on the cook to reheat them or to add more sauce. Courtesy puts someone else's feelings above our own. The least we can do when we are invited to dinner is to try to be on time.

Following these three observations, I found in the margins of Mother's notes another heartfelt thought. "When I cook," she wrote, "I try not to repeat myself but to make a new discovery to improve the basic recipe." Preparing food from scratch is never boring. In a longer notation, she shared this proof of her point: "Once I discovered that it was best never to salt the water when I boiled the corn, because it got tough, I wondered what to do." The answer came in a flash. It's sweet corn! It has to be tender. What works instead is to use a teaspoon of sugar. A chef who never discovers new tricks is usually a bad cook. Mother would agree that when our creativity diminishes in cooking or any other endeavor, everyone suffers.

Prior to the official diagnosis of her Alzheimer's disease, I knew something terribly wrong must be happening to my mother. Her food lacked that extra zip, and so did she. It breaks my heart to remember how I almost dreaded going to dinner at her apartment. I thought for a while it was because of the aging process, but this explanation never satisfied me. After all, aged wine and cheese had exquisite character. What in the world was behind the stiff routine that had taken over in her kitchen? Mother would never have broken her own rule that cooking had to be creative and that boring food was bad.

Wisdom once discovered in a family kitchen deserves to be passed on. "However skilled a chef you become," mother said long before gauges were in vogue, "never guess on the temperature of meat or fowl. Use a meat thermometer. Turn off the oven at least ten minutes before you are ready to remove the roast. Keep the pan warm by covering it with aluminum foil. The roast can stay in the stove for up to thirty minutes, but watch that gauge. Meat should not be treated like shoe leather nor should it be too bloody for human beings to consume!" It's impossible to forget the prime rib roasts she made on special holidays such as Christmas. They were so tasty, so tender, medium with a warm, pink center, a crusty outer rim, and an incredible, mouthwatering aroma.

To take the first bite of something so good was to know with certitude that one was about to embark on a memorable dining experience. Everything on the plate blended together perfectly: the garlicky mashed potatoes, the homemade gravy, the buttery, crunchy peas, the sautéed button mushrooms with imported fennel seeds—it was all so delicious. She herself used to joke, "I'll be dead and gone one of these days, but you'll still remember this meal." How right she was. My mouth waters when I think of it. Her spirituality was forever imprinted on my vitality.

Baking bread told a similar story. First she analyzed like a creative scientist what caused its literal downfall, then she experimented with her findings and produced the recipe most likely to meet her own stringent taste tests. Those were the "good old days" when our family bonded over bread, freshly baked, hot from the oven, coated with real butter, eaten as is or dipped in extra virgin olive oil with a dash of aged balsamic vinegar and freshly grated Parmesan cheese. Ours was a living encounter with the staff of life from which we learned many vital and spiritual lessons.

Mother outlined the following list of possible causes for bread's ruin: The dough will not raise properly if the yeast is old or softened in water that is too hot. "Why kill off a perfectly good ingredient," she would ask with a coy smile, "when the best life has to offer is no more than a trick or two away?" Bread "streaks" if it is under-kneaded. Her reasoning process went like this: Texture has to be taken into account, in food, and in all other relationships. Testing the look and feel of our togetherness, making sure there are no "streaks" in it, is more important than wasting time waiting to see if it has already been ruined.

Moisten the yeast at the last minute or the bread will drop. Mother observed that in cooking as well as in life, timing is everything. "Sometimes we need to moisten our exchanges with uninterrupted listening, with little encouraging hugs. Such gestures are never a waste of time; they contribute to our well-being." We do not want to drop through the cracks of life. We want to rise, not fall.

Perhaps our bodies, more than we would like to admit, are like bread. God, the great mystery, became embodied in his Son, Jesus Christ. He saved us from sin when he submitted his corpus to the cross. It is as destructive to create a false dichotomy between body and soul as it is to deny that Jesus Christ is fully human and fully divine. It would be as foolish for a believer to do so as it would be to try to bake bread without flour. A loaf may be leavened or unleavened, but no bread can be made without that most staple of all ingredients: flour. We would not be spirits without our bodies and our bodies would be merely chemical compounds without our spirits. The lesson here may be that taking the bread of life in Holy Communion satisfies our spiritual hunger like loaves of good home-baked bread nourish our physical needs.

Do not crowd the loaves in the oven; give them space to breathe. "We all need space," she would say. "When we do not give room to one another, we cannot grow. In a way we are like loaves of bread: we need to be 'kneaded' (sorry!)." Our bodies and souls, I thought, by comparison, benefit from times of solitude and silence. Some private place we can call our own, even a corner of the bedroom, is a blessing for our whole organism. We feel more relaxed, less strident, strict, and rigid. We are more likely to flow with grace than to fight against ourselves and God.

Mother's holistic approach to food, her sense of mixing flavors and colors to make supper a celebration of the spirit came to my attention when I found in the next layer of her mementoes an intriguing choice of menus for my youngest brother Victor and his wife Maria's first wedding anniversary. All included a first course, an entree, fresh bread or crescent rolls, dessert, and coffee, complemented by the proper wine and after-dinner cordials.

I do not remember which menu Victor and Maria chose, but each of them would have been scrumptious, perfectly executed, well-balanced, and an unforgettable treat on such a splendid occasion. The ingredients would have been fresh, not frozen or preprocessed, purchased on time, and made that day. Most of the shopping would have been done in the open-air market in Pittsburgh known as the "Strip District." Basil, garlic, fresh ground pepper, and extra virgin olive oil never left her kitchen.

There was a story connected with almost everything mother cooked. Take the filet mignon. When her favorite Italian butcher saw her walk into his shop, he said before she could, "I know, I know, prime not choice, marbled but almost no fat, trimmed lean, one-and-one-half-inch thick, aged and tender, or, in your words, Helen, 'I'll kill you!'" He got the message before she delivered it. Mother was not known for her shyness when it came to ordering any item that would appear on her table; it had to be top notch.

The story goes that the second butcher, a kind of apprentice to her old friend, made eyes at the old butcher's wife one day. Rumor has it that the missing little finger on his left hand had been chopped off "accidentally" when they were making hot sausage. No one could prove otherwise. All I know is that we avoided eating the sausage for a while! Mother laughed until the tears flowed down her cheeks: "Never let it be said that Italians are not passionate about their food." Sausage sales, it seems, were off that whole year, but the story had a happy ending. The apprentice learned his trade; the butcher and his wife became models of fidelity; and the shop began to advertise "Gourmet Sausage for those Great Moments."

There were many recipes Mother never bothered to transcribe. She simply executed them from heart and expected us, her "apprentices," to do the same. When I try to duplicate these recipes, they bring all of my senses to life: the sight of extra-large white moonlight mushrooms; the sound of them sizzling under the broiler; the texture of their cooked and uncooked flesh; the aroma of the special mixture with which they were stuffed; the taste of that pungent blend of spices, pimento peppers, lump crabmeat, fresh breadcrumbs, and a dash of Harvey's Bristol Cream Sherry.

The wild, earthy tones of those oversized caps retained their full flavor with simple stuffing added to them, such as her mixture of their finely diced stems with seasoned Italian bread cubes, chopped parsley, basil, and garlic. She squished the mixture together with one egg, salt and freshly ground pepper, olive oil, and two heaping tablespoons of grated Parmesan or Romano cheese. She finished off these tasty sensations with a dash of paprika. Then into the oven they went for a brief bake and a top crust broil prior to serving.

No wonder when she asked what we wanted for a special treat, she already knew the answer. Her twice-baked potatoes were a splendid complement for any meat, fowl, or seafood entree. Once the six Idahos were baked, cut in half, and gently cleaned out, leaving the skins intact, she would mix them with a half-pound of butter, four tablespoons of sour cream and the same amount of soft cream cheese, followed by a few spoons of heavy whipping cream. Added in were salt, pepper, one large chopped garlic clove, a handful of shredded sharp cheddar cheese, and a tablespoon or so of chopped fresh parsley. Back went this luscious mixture into the potatoes' skins. She'd sprinkle the tops with paprika for color, then put them under the broiler for five minutes before serving.

Mother hated pale food. She used spices for zest and decorated dishes as if they were a canvas on which to paint a masterpiece. I used to stand by and watch her throw together a salad of baby spinach leaves, thin-sliced zucchini, shredded carrots, a bit of lemon juice, the ubiquitous garlic clove, a spoon of capers, a sprinkle of olive oil, a dash of balsamic vinegar, and whatever condiments she liked (notably crushed pepper-corns, sea salt, basil, and oregano), all with a light touch.

Just as it takes the fulfillment of a few good rules to live a wise and balanced human and spiritual life, so must one apply the same principle to food. In mother's kitchen it was always proper:

- To peel the asparagus to guarantee its tenderness.
- To be sure pasta was al dente, never overcooked ("there is no excuse for a mushy noodle!").
- To make bouillon with fresh beef ribs whenever possible.
- To smell and poke the flesh of the fish to be sure it's fresh ("cook with your nose and use your fingers").
- To never serve soggy, overcooked vegetables ("they must be green and crisp or else you might as well throw them on the compost pile.")
- To stick to basic wines like a good Chianti or chardonnay, and be vigilant so that your guests do not drink too much ("it kills their taste buds").

These rules were as humorous as they were to her points of honor. She saw them as avenues to a greater good. She taught me that a godly heart can usually be found in a person who eats good food in moderation. A balanced diet is the key to inner harmony. It proves that a single invitation, such as, "let's eat" aligns our vitality with our spirituality, our heads with our hearts. It keeps body and soul together for another day, proving beyond the shadow of a doubt the formative power of good food.

By contrast, as St. Thomas Aquinas (1225–1274) reminds us, "Irrational feeding darkens the soul and makes it unfit for spiritual experiences."[3] Gluttonous overeating is as harmful to our organism as willful starvation. After all, it is this same Doctor of the Church and author of the *Summa Theologica*, who said in a lighthearted moment, "Sorrow can be alleviated by a good sleep, a bath and a glass of wine."

Food for Thought

When David had finished offering the burnt offerings and the offerings of well-being, he blessed the people in the name of the LORD of hosts, and distributed food among all the people, the whole multitude of Israel, both men and women, to each a cake of bread, a portion of meat, and a cake of raisins. Then all the people went back to their homes. (2 Samuel 6:18–19)

My friend and mentor, Father Adrian van Kaam, related an unforgettable moment he experienced during his time of hiding to escape the Nazi occupiers in Holland during the infamous Hunger Winter of 1944–1945. Along with other "under divers" as they were called, he found refuge in small farms and villages around The Hague where he helped to find what little food there was and delivered it clandestinely to family members and neighbors. One night he and eleven other underground workers gathered in the barn of a friendly farmer to exchange news of the day in the hope of staving off the hunger that gripped them all.

Suddenly a young compatriot joined them. They grew silent and watched as he took from one deep pocket of his trousers a gnarled potato. From the other pocket he extracted a knife, moved to the center of the group, and atop an overturned box proceeded to cut the potato into twelve pieces, reserving one small end for himself. He distributed a bite to everyone, asked the young seminarian among them to bless their food, and with a reverence one could feel in the air, everyone ate. It was, as Father Adrian said, the "eucharist of everydayness."

Sparse as the meal was, it enabled the group to sleep in peace. It was as if their hunger had been relieved in a miraculous way. On that blessed night, greed was overcome by generosity. One potato proved that Divine Providence was with them and that they were safe tonight in God's presence.

Years after the war and after he had survived a devastating heart attack, Father Adrian shifted from a Dutch diet, which featured a lot of dairy products such as butter and cheese, to a Mediterranean diet focusing, as my family taught him, on fresh vegetables and olive oil. One dish of which he grew fond reminded him of his travels in Tuscany. Think of this Italian Bread Salad (recipe below) as sunshine on a plate.

Thoughtful Food
While salads do appear in the family of greens (with a variety of lettuces like red leaf, Bibb, romaine, and arugula), the one that follows eschews members of the lettuce family and takes you in the direction of a leisurely lunch under an arbor of grapes in Tuscany or in an obscure but charming village in Calabria. Here's what you need to assemble your Italian Bread Salad.

Succulent Salad

- 3 finely chopped garlic cloves
- 1 diced sweet or red onion
- 1 medium red bell pepper, cut bite-sized
- 3 stalks of celery, sliced thin
- 1 packet of baby carrots each cut in half
- 1 small thinly sliced baby zucchini
- 4 to 6 ripe plum tomatoes, cubed
- 4 oven-toasted ciabatta rolls cut into bite-sized pieces or 2 cups of cubed focaccia bread lightly toasted
- ¼ cup of chopped fresh parsley
- ¼ cup of fresh basil
- ¼ cup of capers
- ¼ cup of diced, roasted red peppers, a good canned brand

Toss all of these ingredients in a serving bowl, mixing flavors and juices. Add freshly ground sea salt and black pepper to taste. Toss again with the juice of half a lemon, freshly squeezed. Add a half-cup of extra virgin olive oil and two tablespoons of aged balsamic vinegar, followed by a pinch or two of dried oregano. Stir in a quarter-cup of crumbled Gorgonzola cheese. Chill the salad before serving (on chilled plates with chilled forks, if you'd like—a special touch) and sprinkle an additional teaspoon of Gorgonzola cheese atop each plate. Decorate each serving with a sprig of fresh basil. Taste a bit of Tuscany while you enjoy your salad with a glass of Chianti.

Chapter Three

Clean Your Plate

Once on the verge of company arriving and food preparation in full swing, I asked Mother why she objected so much to the idea of appetizers. What was the reason? Quickly she replied, "If guests come to the table without an appetite, why bother to cook at all?" She instructed us to forgo this ritual and simply begin with a first-course option like soup or salad. Once her guests started to eat, no one had to coax them to stay at the table and clean their plates. To this day, no matter in what restaurant I reserve a table, I find myself passing up the appetizer section of a menu and going to the main features or the chef's selections.

Cooking food made from scratch and eating it with gusto is a totally sensual and spiritual experience, moving us from the gratification of a biological need to the joy enkindled by beautiful plating and happy companionship. Mother believed that seeing, smelling, hearing, tasting, and touching food for the body was good for the soul. That is why she cooked with the finesse of the true artist she was. Her food looked as good as it tasted. She gave as much attention to presentation as to flavor.

Spinach puffs, served with a first-course consommé, were light as a feather, and crisp as cracker crust, with a warm fawn color that complemented their leafy green filling. To make them she separated two large eggs, then whisked into the yolks a pinch of salt, a few turns of freshly ground black pepper, a tablespoon of coarsely chopped Italian parsley, and a generous tablespoon of shredded Parmesan cheese. Into this egg mixture she folded three tablespoons of all-purpose flour and one teaspoon of baking powder, forming a smooth batter. After refrigerating it for an hour or so, she would beat the egg whites until they peaked and then fold them into the batter.

In the meantime, she brought to frying temperature two cups of cooking oil (sunflower, canola, or vegetable). She had already washed and dried twenty to twenty-five large leaves of spinach and had stirred them gently into the batter. Then, spoon by spoon, she dipped the coated leaves into the hot oil and fried them to a puffy, golden brown. Once lifted from the frying pan with a slotted spoon, the spinach puffs were drained on paper towels and served immediately with a sprinkle of Parmesan. They could be dipped in horseradish sauce or simply served with a squeeze of lemon. The plate on which they rested pleased the eye of the beholder, and their aroma awakened one's appetite.

Green was a key color in keeping with my mother's aesthetic sensibility. In fact, were there such a reality as the "spirituality" of color, I believe at the top of her list she might have placed green, the reason being that "it's the color of hope." When we think of energizing, vitamin-rich food, green immediately comes to mind. We see in our imaginations a tropical forest inundated with ferns of every shape and color. We like the feel of our toes on soft grass and the twirling of vines between our fingers.

Green makes us inhale deeply as when we sniff a field freshly mown. It makes the air seem more oxygenated, brisk, and clean. It awakens our senses. It makes us remember our dependence on growing things that are alive with nutrients, not dead, overly processed food but items bursting with freshness.

We were a family of "munchers," who liked to chew on leafy romaine lettuce, stalks of celery, baby spinach, arugula, and basil or mint leaves. No matter what we cook or eat green enhances our senses. I remember with joy bright batches of braised kale quickly boiled and then sautéed in olive oil and garlic, with a dash of sea salt and some fresh ground pepper, complemented perhaps by a few red chili pepper flakes. A bowl of this mixture is beautiful to behold and delicious to eat with crusty home-baked bread.

Green goes with any dish. Its versatility is complemented by what is sweet, such as mint, or tart, such as dill, a favorite spice Mother sprinkled on crunchy sugar snap peas. Dandelions picked in yards near and far from our house, blanched and sautéed, tasted best when dusted with imported Romano cheese before serving.

Mother's idea of a fun trip was to take me to the farmer's market where the array of salad greens, pole beans, artichokes, asparagus, and broccoli proved her point: "We were created in a garden and we had better never forget it." Her test to ascertain if we were in a good or bad restaurant never changed: "You can judge the rest of the dinner by the salad. If the greens are limp and pale, what follows will probably be a bad meal. They need to be dark and lush, not drowned in bottled dressing." If the salad was of the highest quality, she predicted that the main course would be the same, "so get ready to give the waiter a big tip."

Greens were like faithful friends. You could count on them to comfort you any season of the year. For Mother, a joyful time of table together-ness began with a plate of greens. Who of us, after a long dark winter, does not welcome seeing those first shoots of spring green? They make us feel that death-to-life thrill that goes beyond words. Our energy returns. Our spirits perk up. We can't wait to plan our first picnic of the year.

Cooking with greens seemed to create a kind of intimacy in the kitchen where we laughed and chatted nonstop while crafting spinach puffs, chopping fresh basil, or making escarole or pea soup to warm us from head to toe on a cold day. What a delight it was to look forward to drinking mint juleps on a hot summer's day. In a green world, it was impossible to lose hope. Nature's hue gave us the option of eating vegetables raw or cooked, but not overcooked. Greens had to stay green.

This was a great art Mother demanded that we perfect. Sautéed spinach had to be as bright as when it came from the grocer's. Asparagus was ruined the minute it turned brown. Beans had to keep their snappy color. Broccoli was beautiful when it looked both steamed and freshly picked at the same time. Then one could admire these greens before eating them. It was this slight pause of admiration that made the difference between eating to live and living to eat.

"If God has a color," Mother would tease, "why should it be bland like khaki and not bright like green?" Think about it. A cactus makes the driest desert look more livable. An old rock overgrown with moss has more character than gray gravel. Even mildew in the cracks of a sidewalk suggests that life forms are stronger than deadly pesticides. When we run across dew-covered grass and climb trees to hide in their leaves, we feel young again, vibrant and full of hope.

Edible greens grow all around our planet. When drought deadens the harvest, people soon die. Green is the food chain's gift to us. On almost any table some green thing can be counted on to complete or complement the meal. This color is not only edible; it has liturgical significance. In my Roman Catholic tradition, the color of the stole worn by the priest in Ordinary Time is green. As the world marks another year from Christmas onward, the central color is green, not blue or yellow, purple or pink. Under the tree we celebrate Christ's birth as a new beginning, even as we await the springtime. Trails of ivy, holly bushes, and window wreaths, all symbolize the hope of the season.

Other colors graced our kitchen like rainbows and changed with the seasons. A dozen eggs hard-boiled and firm as white, packed snow waited in a basket for us to decorate at Easter time. The red wine that filled our glasses to the rim was a reminder of the saving blood of Jesus Christ that washes away our sins and makes us whiter than snow.

A humble color, not to be forgotten when cooking really good food, is brown like the feathers of little sparrows, who do not fall to the ground without our Father knowing it. From collections of dead twigs and dried-up leaves, birds weave lovely nests. If colors had a smell, brown would be earthy and pungent like mushrooms, which turn from beige to burnt umber when they are pickled, breaded, and fried or baked.

In addition to kitchen staples like basil, garlic, fresh parsley, red peppers, leafy dark greens, and crusty breads, our kitchen had to be well stocked with these denizens of dark caves. These wrinkled, dirt-grown delights could be sliced in salads, diced in sauces, sautéed with poultry (as in Chicken Piccata), with meat (as in Veal Marsala), or eaten on their own as a side dish. "A mushroom does not have to be dull," Mother said as she washed and sliced a pound of white buttons and put them in a one-quart mason jar.

Then she combined the following ingredients in a stainless-steel pan and simmered them for fifteen minutes: a cup of dry white wine, one-third cup of extra virgin olive oil, one-and-a-half teaspoons of salt, and a pinch each of black pepper and dried oregano. Then she added to the pan two tablespoons each of chopped fresh parsley, finely diced white onion, and one large clove of minced garlic. She squeezed in three tablespoons of fresh lemon juice, followed by a half-cup of white vinegar, a bay leaf, some dill weed, and a tablespoon of sugar. The mixture must not boil, only simmer. Then she poured it over the mushrooms and refrigerated them in a quart-sized container until suppertime. They were ready to eat after a few hours.

We made this treat in the morning because time would tell if it met Mother's standards of color, taste, smell, and "contrast." As far as she was concerned, relationships where opposites did not attract one another did not work—so why should food? Some of her favorite contrasts were: green/brown; sweet/sour; pungent/mild; hot/cool; hard/soft.

Eggplant was another versatile vegetable in the Italian kitchen. "Never mind what it looks like," Mother said, "It tastes wonderful." She extended this advice, too, to any number of relationships, cautioning us never to judge a book by its cover or base the future on first impressions. "Love is like an eggplant; you have to peel off the skin to appreciate what is underneath it." To make pickled eggplant, she would cut the peeled flesh into cubes and pack them into a quart-sized mason jar to which she added a half-cup of white vinegar, a few peeled garlic cloves, salt, two sliced hot peppers, a half-cup of olive oil, and seasoning to taste.

After tightening the cover, she gave the jar a good shake, chilled the contents overnight, and served them as garnish on her favorite lettuce or tomato salad. She told me to inhale the contents of the quart before she sealed it as if she were putting my nose to a precious perfume. As far as I could tell, mother seemed to think that one got a natural high from inhaling marinated mushrooms and eggplant. What drug could compare to that of having all of one's senses satisfied?

In life, as in the art of eating, a key ingredient to happiness is flexibility. Too much rigidity kills the spontaneity of mature faith. In food preparation, this disposition translates into versatility. I believe eggplant was another staple in our kitchen because it was so versatile.

It became many tastes to many palates. Its adaptability meant that each eater could find in it something different to enjoy. Eggplant was, to my mother, as versatile as tofu is in Asian cuisine. It, too, adapts itself to whatever dish it enters—much like a humble servant does what must be done in any situation where a need presents itself.

"Peel and cube those two medium-sized eggplants," she told me. "Use only the solid part and discard the seedy interiors. Let them soak in salt for a while; then rinse them well and put them in that large bowl over there. Add about a cup of this chopped celery. Dice in those plum tomatoes. I've already blanched and peeled them. A cup will do. Chop that red bell pepper into the mixture with one finely sliced shallot, a half-cup of diced black olives, and a quarter-cup of capers. Mix everything together. Add salt and fresh ground pepper to taste. Lightly sauté a cup of sliced mushrooms in olive oil with a couple of crushed garlic cloves and don't let it burn! Add some parsley to the bowl and a few red hot pepper flakes. Now pour what you've cooked over the eggplant mixture. Let's serve this delicacy on garlic toast. It's my version of bruschetta."

That's how I learned to cook. She did not have to convince me what a treat was in store. I watched these ordinary ingredients change into extraordinary taste sensations.

The transformative power of terrific food is depicted in a brilliant Danish film titled *Babette's Feast*. A French woman with a natural knack for gourmet cooking transforms a "sour dough" Danish town full of dour faces into a community dancing under the stars after enjoying the banquet she prepared. Vitality in service of spirituality was a proven formula in Babette's kitchen.

I saw eyes roll with similar pleasure when Mother served a specialty of hers: chopped chicken liver. She learned how to make it when she worked in a clothing store during and after the Depression. She was familiar with the fashion world, and knew how to put herself together with color-coordinated outfits and perfectly coifed hair.

The proprietor of the Fashion Hosiery Shop must have taken one look at her and decided on the spot to hire this inexperienced young lady. The fact that she had never worked in retail did not seem to matter. She said with full certitude, "Put me behind the counter and if I don't make my keep by day's end, fire me!" The boss knew he had nothing to lose. He liked her direct approach, perhaps intuiting that she was not the type to pass up a challenge: "Let's see if you have what it takes to work for me." He pointed to a lady entering the shop with the quick disclosure that she was one of their toughest customers to please.

Several minutes later when the customer left with a big smile on her face, new undergarments, and ten pairs of hosiery, Mother's boss-to-be shook his head in amazement and asked what she had said to her. "Nothing special. We gabbed about recipes and she gave me hers for chopped chicken liver. That was what I wrote in my notes in addition, of course, to her name and address. It turns out we have a lot in common. I told her how to make quick but classy marinara sauce. The purchases were a side benefit of our hitting it off so well. Selling happens fastest when you change the subject." The eyes of her supervisor widened with surprise and pleasure. "That's a secret I thought I would have to teach you, but you know it already. You're a natural." Before long she was the manager of his main store.

Mother always prefaced the preparation of the recipe her customer divulged by telling this story. Whatever transpired between customer and salesperson left both of them the better for it.

Then she told me what to do: "Begin by sautéing two pounds of fresh chicken livers in olive oil and a pat of butter. Cook them thoroughly.

Add a teaspoon of salt and a quarter-teaspoon of black pepper, with the same measure of paprika. Follow up with two tablespoons of rich chicken broth. Add another tablespoon or two of olive oil, followed by a half-teaspoon of dried sage, two tablespoons of chopped onion, fresh parsley and basil. Then add one finely sliced shallot and a large clove of garlic. Pour into this thickened mixture a quarter-cup of cream sherry, a dash of Worcestershire sauce, a quarter-cup of chopped celery, a half-teaspoon of Dijon mustard, a tablespoon of mayonnaise, and four crushed hard-boiled eggs."

She moved at top speed while assembling these ingredients, and I did my best to keep up with her. Finally, all elements of the recipe went into the food processor and out came a fabulous spread that delighted everyone who tasted it on Melba toasts or crisp wheat crackers. Before serving her guests, she would pour herself a small glass of sherry, spread the chilled chicken liver on a piece of toast, and enjoy a special moment reminiscing about the joy she felt in times past sharing this dish at the home of friends.

Without her knowing it, I felt myself stepping across the threshold of whatever keeps us apart. Why not think of food as a factor in promoting world peace? Sit around a table lined with faces representing a diversity of colors and creeds. Set upon it dish after dish of great cuisine and see what happens. No prejudice. No fighting. No killing. No weapons of mass destruction. No terrorism. No name-calling or useless arguments. Instead, we who represent different faith and cultural traditions sit together and enjoy the delicacies each country has to offer. Dinner diplomacy begins. Excellent food and wine complement good conversation. Ours is an experience of oneness in the spirit rooted in the vital substructure provided by a variety of heavenly food. When such banquets are spread before us, foes become friends.

Eating has a transformative effect, providing not only substantial nourishment but also food for thought that connects young and old, women and men, professionals and peasants. Tables of plenty remind us that we share the goods this planet of ours yields moment by moment. When one part of it dies or is despoiled by a natural disaster like the oil spill in the Gulf of Mexico, we all suffer. Something precious in the food chain has been broken and needs to be repaired and restored as soon as possible.

We do not own the earth's abundance; it is a gift from God whose only request is that we treat it gently and share its benefits with perfect generosity. As St. Basil the Great (330–379) once said: "The bread you store up belongs to the hungry; the cloak that lies in your chest belongs to the naked; the gold that you have hidden in the ground belongs to the poor."[4]

Food for Thought

I am the LORD your God,

who brought you up out of the land of Egypt.

Open your mouth wide and I will fill it. (Psalm 81:10)

One of the most touching episodes concerning food for body and soul appears in the first book of Kings (17:7–16). Elijah has been in hiding near a brook that has run dry. The Lord sees his plight and tells him it is time to move on to a place called Zarephath where he will meet a widow chosen by God to provide for his needs. The prophet goes there immediately and, as predicted, encounters a widow at the entrance to the city. We never are told her name, but her fidelity is unforgettable. Elijah sees her gathering sticks to make a little fire. Trusting as he is, he asks her for a cup of water and, as she leaves to get if for him, he begs her to bring with it a bit of bread.

Now the story moves from an interesting narration to the level of a transcendent mystery. The widow confesses that all she has left is a handful of flour in her jar and perhaps a teaspoon of oil in her jug. She has baked nothing yet but once the fire is lit and the dough rises it will be the end of her provisions and she and her son will starve to death. Elijah tells her to fear not, for such is not the way of the Lord. The cake she is about to bake has to be given to him and then she can prepare something for herself and her son to eat. Through the prophet she learns the awesome truth embedded in the gift of sharing the last drop of one's food with a needy other: "The jar of flour shall not go empty, nor the jug of oil run dry…."

So the widow does as Elijah instructed and, as Scripture tells us, she was able to eat for a year, and so were Elijah and her son. In this "loaves and fishes" episode, manifesting the providence of God, food rises to epiphanic proportions, for, as the Lord foretold, the jar of flour did not go empty, nor the jug of oil run dry. When we give from our want, when we open our table to the hungry, the return God makes to us is a wonder to behold.

What strikes us in this story is its emphasis on the biblical notion of comfort. It is the basis of one of the beatitudes of Jesus: "Blessed are those who mourn, for they shall be comforted" (Matthew 5:4). The Lord comforts us in our loss and rewards us for being faithful to him. When we weep, our Beloved dries our tears. When it feels as if we are on the verge of collapse, the Comforter holds our hand. Comfort reminds us that we are not alone. Someone really cares for us like a good cook loves her guests. We come to the table and we do so for free. Another has already paid the price.

Phony words of comfort, like those offered to the poor man Job, have no place here. Expressions of sympathy devoid of genuine empathy only create discomfort. Ours is a need only God can satisfy, for God is "the Father of compassion and the God of all comfort" (2 Corinthians 1:3). With his rod and his staff God comforts us like the Good Shepherd he is (Psalm 23:4). The comfort theme in Scripture soothes the aching soul and leads us to speak with perennial fondness of "comfort food."

Thoughtful Food

Comfort food in my family was synonymous with meatloaf and there is no recipe that fits the bill better than the one "concocted" by my mother (her word).

Into two pounds of lean ground beef placed in a large mixing bowl add one cup of wet bread (preferably Italian) squeezed as dry as possible. Have on hand one cup of mashed potatoes and one cup of ricotta. Add both to the meat and bread mixture. Next break into it four eggs and add a half-cup of heavy cream and the same amount of mayonnaise. Stir and add for color a quarter-cup of ketchup. Knead the whole mixture by hand until all the ingredients are blended. Then season to taste with salt and pepper and a few drops of Worcestershire sauce. Shape into a loaf and place in a nonstick shallow pan to bake at 350° for one hour.

Before serving, let the loaf rest in a wrap of aluminum foil. Prepare a thin sauce with the pan drippings, one teaspoon of cornstarch, and a quarter-cup of Marsala wine. Thicken slowly, unwrap your masterpiece, and drizzle the sauce over it just before serving. You'll already feel comforted by the aroma from the oven. Once you taste it, perhaps with a leafy green side salad with a lemon-pepper dressing, there is no room left for sadness in your whole system.

Chapter Four

Feeding Body and Soul

Every faith journey begins with a story to tell, a formation event to relate, a seedbed of legend to fertilize. Different though we are, we find as storytellers how much we have in common.

Once when I was visiting a village in Tanzania where a student of mine grew up, I was served a plate of roasted pork and vegetables—extra spicy but, for my palate, quite enjoyable. To allay our thirst, our hosts passed around a pot of banana beer. I had never tasted such a brew before but it proved to be irresistible for two reasons: the hospitality with which it was offered and the pleasant taste it left on my tongue.

We sat at a low table and not a bite was consumed without a prayer of blessing being said before each course. I was used to saying a general grace before meals with perhaps a muttered thanksgiving afterwards, but here, where food could be as sparse as it was precious, each serving called for thanks. Whoever came to the village was greeted with servings of whatever the villagers had: solid fare for the body, sincere prayer for the soul. Had a visitor like me refused their offerings because their strange taste was not what I expected, the discourtesy shown would have been shocking. Instead, the meal I shared could not have been better had it been served on a table set with gold-plated china.

Being fed gives us our first clue to what life holds in store. A child nestling safely in its mother's arms senses without a word that the world is a trustworthy place. At the end of life, as when taste buds fail and appetite dwindles, trust in one's caregivers remains an unspeakable grace. From life's start to its finish, significant events are framed by food. As soon as the flow of nourishment to our vital dimension ceases, the life force as we knew it soon wanes away and we breathe our last.

Whether food comes to us in minuscule portions that do not relieve hunger or on plates so full we have to discard half of what's on them, there is no escaping the necessity of eating. Touring the horrific yet holy ground of the Holocaust Museum in Washington, DC, revealed to me just how gruesome a reality death by starvation is. Poisoning a food or water source is an ancient weapon used by tyrants to subdue one person or a whole population. People can also eat themselves to death. Food can be an avenue to life-threatening anorexia or bulimia. It can preserve life or destroy it.

Gluttony is a cardinal sin, and most of us have been exposed to over-indulgence by some while others go hungry. The garbage flung from restaurants in the West could feed whole villages in the developing world. Food becomes an issue when we become obsessed with counting the calories we consume in order to reduce our body weight, not for reasons of health but in the illusion that skeletal thinness is a banner of beauty.

In reflecting on the connection between vitality and spirituality, food in itself is not the problem. What causes harm is our inability to handle and package it safely and then to cook and consume it in a wise and balanced way. We need to read the labels on the products we buy to ascertain, for instance, their fat and sodium and sugar content. Health consciousness is on the increase.

Extending our life expectancy may become more of a reality when we take into account the importance of nutrition and exercise. Amateurs, to say nothing of professional cooks, want to know the difference between bleached white and whole grain bread; how to choose more organic ingredients and eat healthy fruits and vegetables; why it is an honor and a joy to share the plenty we have with the poor who come to our door.

Of all the basic fare we could name, two examples take center stage: bread and water. Given these twin staples, human beings can survive circumstances as dehumanizing as death camps and as depleting as sun-drenched deserts.

When the chosen people found themselves wandering in the desert, they begged God to help them. He did so by giving them water from rocks and manna from heaven. These essentials were living proof of his covenant love. God's only-begotten Son saw a similar need and with a few loaves of bread and some fish fed five thousand people. At the Last Supper, he broke the bread that became his body. The Eucharistic sacrifice is at the heart of our Christian traditions. At this table we partake of a perfectly blended earthly and heavenly banquet.

Bread has a place of honor on many ethnic tables, and certainly the Italian is no exception. It is baked, broken, dipped, and toasted. It is the basis of two greatly loved traditional dishes: bruschetta and pizza. It can be crafted into almost any shape—round, square, twisted: We made bread into rolls or flattened it to form focaccia; we flavored it with nothing more than a pinch of salt or filled it with spices; we moistened it in stuffing, crumbled it to coat chicken and fish, fried it and then smothered it with powdered sugar and raisins to produce a delicious dessert.

No memory of my childhood is more vivid than that of the taste, touch, sight, sound, and smell of freshly baked bread. My grandmother made it almost daily, as did my mother. They passed their love for this dietary delight on to every member of our family. I learned that it was not excellent bread consumed in moderation that made people overweight but pale bread with no nutrients. Mushy white bread made with bleached flour shot full of chemicals was unthinkable on our table. "Read what's in that so-called Wonder Bread," Mother said, "And you'll know why I warned it would ruin your appetite." The aroma of her bread filled the house and sent us flying to the kitchen to eat it with fresh butter the minute it came out of the oven. In due time we learned it was not permissible for us merely to consume it; we had to learn how to make it ourselves. (You'll find a traditional bread recipe on page 110.)

Bread was never reserved for our family alone; it was meant to be shared with friends and neighbors. Tuesday was baking day and they knew it. Holiday breads were especially appreciated and not a scrap was wasted. Bread could be reconstituted into any number of new forms from homemade croutons to turkey stuffing. Bread was also a great teacher of the need to follow rules like: "Wet the yeast with tepid water and make it the last ingredient you add to your mixture." The results of adhering to tested wisdom generated a new echelon of bakers, who knew that dough will not rise properly if the yeast is old or if it is softened in water that is too hot.

Nothing can last if something kills it at the start—be it a budding friendship or a loaf of bread. If the dough is not kneaded enough, it will have an uneven texture, "so don't be afraid to work it thoroughly."

Mother said to think of the process in marital terms: "A couple has to work on building their togetherness every day; otherwise a divorce mentality creeps in before they know it." She also believed firmly as a faithful wife that "the way to a man's heart is through his stomach." That was one of the sayings, however old-fashioned it may sound, by which my mother lived, followed by a close second: "Never try to talk to a man when his stomach is empty."

My father, Frank Muto, confirmed the truth of this declaration with a resolute nod and a broad grin. So much for expensive or lengthy marriage counseling! Yet in all such sayings there resides a grain of truth because they never fail to touch upon the connection between vitality and spirituality: "Take time to baby the bread and it will comfort you." We were taught to think of bread in personal terms. "Like you, it needs tender loving care to be good."

Inherent in these counsels are important lessons as to why good eating is a transformative experience for body and soul. The first rule to produce a good meal is to do what we do with a heart full of love. Wonderful results do not happen in a hurry. Second, we need to bring the ingredients that make up our lives into balance, like the ingredients for making a delicious loaf of bread. Balance is everything: Not too little, not too much. Not too hot, not too cold. Third, we need space in which to grow. Like a bread dough that needs to double in volume, then double again, in order to produce a light, fluffy, and tasty loaf, we need to have the time and space to rise to our full potential. Spoiled bread—sunken, sticky, tasteless—is like a relationship gone sour. Instead of being an experience at once unique and communal, it violates the commandment to respect the dignity of each person and to do unto others what we hope they will do for us.

In fact, baking something as simple as bread has more symbolic value than you might realize. In the Bible, to bake and serve bread signals hospitality, reverence for guests, and gratitude for a God who provides. Remember in the book of Genesis when Abraham said to Sarah, "Make ready quickly three measures of choice flour, knead it, and make cakes" (Genesis 18:6). Here was a morsel of food fit for angels and prepared by human hands—a wonderful example of the wedding of the ordinary and the extraordinary, the natural and the supernatural. Baked goods can be enticements to overindulge, but savory odors arising from the oven can also enkindle joy and lead to modest but satisfying treats.

When a measure of yeast allows bread dough to swell, we can only imagine how faith the size of a mustard seed can blow doubts away like thistles in the wind. Why else would Jesus have said, "The kingdom of heaven is like yeast that a woman took and mixed in with three measures of flour until all of it was leavened" (Matthew 13:33)? This paradox of the miniscule producing a magnitude of divine abundance must never be forgotten by the community of faith. We must consume on a regular basis the "bread of sincerity and truth" (1 Corinthians 5:8).

One of Mother's favorite productions, all of which we ate with gusto, were her egg crescent rolls (see recipe on page 111). These always appeared on our Easter or Christmas table. No holiday would have been complete without them, so good and easy were they to make: "Beat in a large mixing bowl six eggs, six heaping tablespoons of sugar, two teaspoons of salt, one half-cup of warm water, six tablespoons of oil, and a half cake of household yeast dissolved in a little warm water and sugar. Once this mixture is ready, slowly add it to six cups of flour and work the dough well. Then let it rise for an hour or so, punch it down, and let it rise for at least another hour."

Making the crescents was a work of art. Once the dough was punched down and rolled out, it had to be cut into three portions and flattened like a piecrust. Each portion was then cut into six or eight wedges. The thinnest portion was rolled toward the largest, after the flat piece had been lightly buttered. Voila! A perfect half-moon roll was created, then baked, and presented to everyone's "oohs" and "aahs."

The versatility of dough like this never failed to evoke my wonder. To it could be added nuts, raisins, and cinnamon to produce a savory bread perfect for breakfast or a special treat. Like our spiritual life, dough was formed, reformed, and transformed—each time becoming progressively better. Turning flour and water into the staff of life, be it leavened or unleavened, was like becoming a co-creator with our Creator.

Bread making is a distinctly spiritual process—like the dying of one form of life and the rising of another. I would venture to say that in the modern family, whose members are frantically over-scheduled, there may be many good reasons to reinstate the art of bread baking. There is no substitute for the aroma, the taste, the expression of care evident in a freshly baked loaf of bread. Microwaving, however convenient, is no substitute for slow baking.

Although baking bread takes time, it can be a once-a-week event that brings relaxation and pleasure to a family. Children can be involved by being asked to knead the dough or mix the ingredients. The simple process of baking bread can be a balm for overworked minds and stressful lives. Fresh bread offers an incentive to sit at table, break bread together, and celebrate our common humanity. Bread is a reminder of the importance of returning to the basics since our commonality is as ordinary as flour and water. Bread reverses the pain of having become so decentered that we lose awe for the mystery that embraces us like the protective crust around a loaf.

The secret to a good first course, the intermezzo between the salad and the main entrée, was that it be light but substantial, that it leave room for the next course but be solid enough that if one wanted to stop there one could. The answer in our family was either great bread or pasta or, frankly, the two together. Pasta did not necessarily mean heavy noodles with cheese sauces. Neither did it move in the direction of sticky macaroni with globs of chopped meat. Rather it was both feathery and al dente, most likely cappellini (angel hair) or penne with a "fresh as a spring garden" marinara sauce, coating the pasta but not drenching it, perhaps leaving just enough at the bottom of the plate for cleaning it with a bit of bread—a great compliment to the cook.

Preparing the sauce was like entering into a liturgical ceremony. We had to follow a certain ritual. Into the oiled and "rubbed with garlic" sauce pot, heated on medium flame (later to be lowered to simmer) would be poured a large can of high quality imported tomato puree, followed by one can of slighted diluted tomato paste, a half-dozen diced, seeded, blanched, and peeled plum tomatoes, a quarter-cup of Chianti or other dry red wine and, if the sauce needed to be further diluted, we were not to use water but some tomato juice. In a side pan we would sauté in extra virgin olive oil one diced onion, a few finely chopped garlic cloves, and salt and pepper to taste. To these ingredients would be added several sprigs of chopped fresh basil and parsley, a half-teaspoon or so of red pepper flakes and a tablespoon of capers. This savory mixture would be added to the simmering tomatoes and be allowed to cook slowly for a few hours.

Just before it was time to serve the first course, the table would be cleared, large deep dishes would appear, the pasta would have reached the ideal consistency and so the sauce, with freshly grated Romano and Parmesan cheese added to it, would go on the pasta that had been drained well. All was in readiness for us as we eagerly awaited the first forkful. For one imaginary moment it was as if we were transported to that small village in Calabria whence my people immigrated to America. The steamy pasta, the pungent smell of the cheese, the hot, buttered bread, a sampling of my grandfather's vintage wines and, in the blink of an eye, we had flown from our street to those sunny Italian shores.

Pasta marinara had only one serious rival at our family table and that would have been Mother's fettuccini Alfredo, a dish she first tasted, she said, while on vacation in Atlantic City in 1935. Her take on what she tasted was to ready a half-pound of fettuccini to the point of perfection (her timing for pasta was flawless) while heating in a nonstick saucepan a half-cup of melted butter, a half-cup of heavy cream, one cup of freshly grated Parmesan cheese, some fresh parsley, a pinch of salt, and a generous dash of ground pepper. This simple combination tasted wonderful when poured over the pasta and topped with a bit more cheese. Another version was to add to the same mixture a chopped garlic clove, a tablespoon or so of olive oil, a half-cup of grated mozzarella cheese, some oregano, and a teaspoon of cream sherry. That, too, was divine!

Flavors are essential, not extraneous, when one aims to prepare food that sits well not only in our stomachs but also in our memories. One day I stood in the doorway of the kitchen and waved to Mother not to mind me but to continue her preparation for what she named "Pasta Helen." Egg noodles were her choice for the base of this Romanoff-style dish. She stood at the stove sautéing several cloves of chopped garlic, and one cup each of diced red, green, and yellow peppers, in a quarter-cup of olive oil, to which she added fresh parsley and basil. With the fire on low she folded into these ingredients a cup of sour cream, a quarter-cup of grated Romano, a tablespoon of chives, a teaspoon of salt, a half-teaspoon of black pepper, and two tablespoons of butter. When the entire mixture had reached the boiling point, she poured it over the cooked noodles, sprinkled them with Parmesan and paprika and there it was—a dish fit for Russian royalty but offered to an ordinary family—from Helen with love.

I learned that when desperation set in and I did not know what to cook I could always fall back on what she dubbed "Fettuccini Pronto." It could be done in an electric wok set at 325°. After pouring some olive oil down the sides of the wok and into the center, we added chopped sweet onions and sliced garlic, julienned red pepper, a small hot pepper, a cup of sliced baby zucchini, two cups of tender precooked broccoli florets, and several chopped leaves of fresh mint (a great touch). All ingredients were stir-fried and seasoned with salt and pepper. Then we added a cup of sliced fresh mushrooms and a half-cup of sliced black olives. This wonderful vegetarian mixture was cooked for another ten minutes, then topped with a handful of freshly chopped basil and parsley.

The pasta was put on to boil and at the precise moment drained and added to what we had prepared already. At the last minute, Mother added a half-cup of vermouth, a half-cup of cream, and a similar amount of grated Parmesan complemented by six ounces of brick cheese, all of which was stirred into the wok. The liquid portion was thickened with a bit of diluted cornstarch topped off with three tablespoon of pignoli (pine nuts). When everything was assembled on a large serving platter I knew we had created an edible work of art. All who ate it left the table feeling happier than when they sat down. Food is a gift, and we were drawn together as its worthy recipients.

Flavor, it seems to me, is as much at the vital center of food as faith is at the heart of every religious experience. We can reproduce pretend flavors by combining the right chemicals, but the consequences can damage our taste for the real thing. People think that by choosing low-fat ingredients they will lose weight, but the opposite may be true if they do not examine the sugar content of the product. Food was not meant to be artificial, no more than people are meant to become chronic liars. Good food, to say nothing of good consumers of it, depends on what is on the inside. Clever affectations are as unconvincing to discerning eyes as fake colors are in food.

Some people with health concerns—diabetes, high cholesterol, food allergies—must be careful about what they eat. You may need to substitute ground turkey for ground beef in your meatballs, or make substitutions to accommodate for food sensitivity. Yet even with that, wholesome, well-prepared food, eaten in moderation, is what keeps us healthy.

"How do you stay in shape?" people used to ask Mother when they saw the abundance on her table. "Weight gain," she would reply, "has nothing to do with the food we eat or the ingredients we use; it has to do with the quantity we consume. If you eat too much, your weight will rise. One decent portion of lasagna satisfies your hunger, but three portions will blow you up like a balloon." Her philosophy of food kept her at a healthy weight even when Alzheimer's claimed her memory and she had no choice but to bite into mashed preparations until that, too, became impossible.

The filling she layered on lasagna noodles was rich but, eaten in moderation, this recipe was so pleasing to the palate that no one ever needed to overeat to feel satisfied. She started with two pounds of whole ricotta into which she stirred a mixture of imported grated cheeses like Fontinella, Asiago, and provolone to which she added a cup of cream, three eggs, a half-cup of sifted flour, eight ounces of softened cream cheese, a pound of grated mozzarella, three tablespoons of olive oil, chopped parsley and basil, a teaspoon of salt, and a dash of cinnamon (her secret ingredient). If the mixture needed to be thickened she recommended adding to it two tablespoons of diluted cornstarch. The cooked noodles were layered in a large casserole with her favorite tomato sauce (meatless or with meat) and topped with a sprinkling of Parmesan. The casserole baked for about an hour at 350°, and the result was so good all her friends requested the recipe.

Enjoying a special dish like this drew people together in a bond of happiness many miss in the fast lanes where we live. A meal shared with gusto guarantees that we want to see one another again around the table. Repeat performances are the test of how much we enjoy being together. Sharing good food strengthens the bond of friendship. We become more sensitive to our likes and dislikes, more alert to what stops or advances the flow of conversation interrupted by smiles and hearty laughter. Glum faces usually signal dull food, lacking flavor and provoking no interest in second helpings.

If there was one lesson we learned early in life, it was that at our table the taste of food mattered a lot. The din of dishes being passed and tested for their flavor, the pitch of people trying to outshout one another, was like background music in an Italian movie. The overall impression that stays with me is one of joy—*la dolce vita!* Once, during my teenage years, I accepted a dinner invitation from the family of a classmate of mine. The conversation around the table was as bright as the food was bland, but no one seemed to notice that but me.

The mood at the end of the meal was rather somber because we had been discussing weighty world issues with nothing tasty to offset them. I missed the smell of fresh garlic and basil. To me these staples were like some ancient elixir capable of curing ill will. I liked the witty exchanges but left the table feeling hungry because second helpings were encouraged but held no incentive.

An unspoken but felt lack of satisfaction both bodily and spiritually causes eaters to crave more food to comfort a disappointed palate. But more in quantity does not mean satisfaction due to quality. Over the years, I watched the faces of childhood friends who seemed tired and depressed brighten considerably when they came home with me to dinner. If food done right and taken in balanced proportions could be compared to medicine, then I witnessed many cures. Homemade gnocchi softened hardened hearts and quieted fears over reporting bad grades to one's parents. Manicotti featuring paper-thin crepes stuffed with a feather-light mixture of cheeses seemed to reduce tension in teenagers and adults. I saw food turn sullen silence into friendly banter. People who hardly ever prayed asked us to say thanksgiving after a meal, not only a blessing before it, because they felt so satisfied.

Whenever I needed to see the world and my purpose in it in a new light, I would whip up Mother's linguine with clam sauce and inevitably life looked brighter. Maybe this was a case of mind over matter but so what? For red sauce, sauté some olive oil and a dab of butter with minced garlic, onion, chopped celery, bits of pepper flakes, parsley, a touch of oregano, and a teaspoon each of basil and thyme. Add some chopped fresh plum tomatoes, two tablespoons of sherry, and two cans of drained minced clams. Cook for about thirty minutes (some of the liquid should evaporate) and pour over the linguini.

The red sauce, Mother claimed, quelled anger; the white sauce lifted one's spirits. For that experience, follow the same steps as above only skip the tomatoes and add instead a half-cup of dry and another half-cup of sweet white wine. To thicken the mixture stir in two table-spoons of soft, silky flour and enjoy a prime example of soul food.

The right pasta with a perfectly matched sauce can complement any entree. Try spaghetti with anchovies and chickpeas. Be inventive because when spirits soar stomachs follow, and vice versa. When stomachs are full, spirits follow. Pasta is neither picky nor judgmental. It loves to be coated with pesto sauce (green), cheese sauce (white), tomato sauce (red), or mushrooms (brown). Use your imagination and let go of every trace of culinary uptightness. Fresh pasta (never canned or trapped in a carton) can be served warm, hot, or cold, as in a salad. It is as adaptable as we should be. In moderation it is an excellent source of carbohydrates. Being a good addition to almost any meal, it qualifies for the family feeling of satisfaction really good food deserves to receive.

Food for Thought
Better is a dinner of vegetables where love is
than a fatted ox and hatred with it. (Proverbs 15:17)

During the time she worked at the Fashion Hosiery Shop, Mother received several invitations to Sabbath meals and Passover celebrations. It occurred to her that socializing with Jews might not be in keeping with the Church's teaching in those pre–Vatican II times. During her lunch hour one day, she slipped into the nearest church to go to confession. After telling her story, the priest refused to give her absolution unless she stopped accepting these invitations and gave a firmer witness to her Catholic faith.

With rapt attention, I asked her how she felt and what she did. With typical spunk, she told me she did not feel right about this harsh counsel and decided to walk to another nearby church. There she found in the confessional an old Italian priest. He listened to her concerns and then told her that he, too, loved Jewish people because Jesus was a Jew, and that a key element in the practice of her Catholic faith was to show love for everyone. He absolved her of her other sins and at the end of the sacrament asked her with a tremor in his voice if she knew where he—who had recently come to Pittsburgh from New York—could find an authentic corned beef sandwich. Of course, she knew the perfect address, and penitent and priest left the sanctuary on a jolly note. How could I have gotten a better lesson in interreligious tolerance than from this humane and charming food story?

Thoughtful Food

This recipe for deviled crab cakes (see page 117), satisfying to any guest who graced our dinner table when I was growing up, was invented by my mother and is a winner for any seafood lover. It begins when you sauté, in a quarter-cup of olive oil and a tablespoon of butter, a small, finely chopped Vidalia onion; two chopped garlic cloves; a diced red sweet pepper; and a quarter-cup each of chopped fresh parsley and chives. As the first stage of cooking completes itself, add in, stirring constantly, two tablespoons of flour and, slowly poured, one cup of milk, one-third cup of melted Swiss cheese, and a quarter-cup of mayonnaise.

As this mixture begins to bubble gently, add to it one tablespoon of freshly squeezed lemon juice, one tablespoon of brandy, and a teaspoon of lemon zest. Seasonings now include a few drops of Tabasco sauce and the same of Worcestershire plus a teaspoon of chili pepper flakes. Put the flame on simmer.

In a separate bowl beat one egg and stir it into the sauce until thoroughly blended. After that fold in a quarter-cup of grated Italian cheese (a combination of Romano and Parmesan). If necessary, thicken the sauce with some cornstarch. Now add to it two cups of tightly packed lump crabmeat (buy the best!). Distribute the blended crab mixture into eight crab cake molds and sprinkle each with buttered and toasted breadcrumbs. Refrigerate your molds until just before serving time. Then bake them on a flat pan for approximately twenty-five minutes at 350°.

Finish them off under the broiler for a few moments to turn the crust golden and serve the molds with a generous helping of peeled asparagus dressed with olive oil, garlic, butter, and dill weed. Balance the table with some garlic bread sticks and a chilled white wine like Sauvignon Blanc or a sparkling wine like Prosecco. Expect to hear a satisfying litany of "Yum-yum!"

Chapter Five

Complements and Main Courses

Eating balanced meals takes you one step closer to living a balanced life. At our table, carbohydrates had to be complemented by a source of protein, be it meat, poultry, or fish. Mother loved fillet of sole fresh from the seafood market. She preferred a simple preparation, consisting of olive oil, butter, garlic, parsley, dill, and lemon to bring out the natural flavors of the fish. She did not coat the fillets with any heavy sauces; they always signaled to her that the fish was a day old and needed a cover story! If fish is really fresh, why alter its appearance with a "foreign element" that changes its flavor? Her preference in food always veered in the direction of lightness. This rule applied to vegetables, which, she said, "had to be treated like the fresh flowers displayed with beauty and delicacy in the table's centerpiece."

When Mother started to prepare her cauliflower casserole, it was as if an outdoor garden had come inside the kitchen. Like sun bursting through the clouds on a rainy day, it was a dish that brought a smile to her face although she knew her memory was beginning to play a few tricks on her. Her first task was to boil a large, trimmed, clean head in salted water until it was white and tender. Atop it she drizzled a quarter-cup of melted butter and the same portion of garlic-infused olive oil.

Into a pan set over medium heat, she added some heavy cream, a half-teaspoon of salt, and her favorite seasonal herbs. She then stirred into the liquid that reached the boiling point a half-cup of shredded cheddar cheese, a quarter-cup of sour cream, a teaspoon of Dijon mustard, and a dash of Worcestershire sauce. She broke the cooked cauliflower into chunks laid out in a large, flat glass dish and poured this rich sauce over it. She covered her creation with a half-cup of coarse breadcrumbs and a quarter-cup of diced sweet red pepper. Then it went into the oven to bake at 325° for about forty minutes under a sheet of aluminum foil. Just before serving this special dish of hers as a complement to lemon-scented roasted chicken or a fennel-flavored pork loin, she crisped the top under the broiler. The cauliflower casserole was only rivaled by another vegetable preparation of hers we loved—baked zucchini.

To make it, she grated three or four unpeeled zucchinis—enough to yield six to eight cups—of the freshest ones we could find at the farmer's market. All excess moisture had to be squeezed out. "The drier the better," she said. To these green-and-white mounds we added minced sweet onion, one diced red and one green pepper, a grated potato and a cup of shredded carrots. Everything had to be mixed well together before we drizzled in a half-cup of olive oil, a quarter-cup of melted butter, one cup of sour cream, a quarter-cup of mayonnaise, and a half-cup of heavy cream. Salt and pepper, basil and parsley, and coarsely cut garlic cloves were used to season the mixture, which she then topped with a cup of breadcrumbs and the same portion of mixed grated cheeses. Into the oven it went in an oiled and floured casserole to bake for one hour at 325°. The casserole was mated at table with savory baked chicken or char-grilled flank steak.

Remembering these meals evokes not only gratitude but regret that we often took them for granted. Did I thank Mother enough for preparing them? Did I tell her how much they contributed to the formation of my character—bodily and spiritually? We probably had so many eating highs at home that, without realizing it, neither drugs nor alcohol were ever an issue. We were too busy running to the table to relish home-cooked meals to worry about getting into trouble. Food prepared with love is basic to our well-being. No wonder its consumption begins and ends with a blessing. Life's meaning risks being lost when we settle for poor, carelessly prepared or hurried nutrition. This loss is not only physical; it entails a lack of companionship with others and ultimately with God.

To this day when I need to add that extra special touch to the table for the sake of pleasing my guests, I turn to one of these tried-and-true recipes of Mother's—crafted not scientifically but spontaneously, leaving ample room for improvisation and improvement. For whatever reason I associate what follows with this free-flowing cooking style: "Boil four yams until they are soft and cooled enough to peel them. Then slice them into an elongated dish already buttered. Now add to the same dish four cooked carrots sliced thickly. Cover the dish with a can of crushed pineapple. Add to it some freshly grated orange and lemon peel and the juice of one fresh orange. Now mix together a quarter-cup of light corn syrup, a teaspoon of diluted cornstarch, a quarter-cup of sugar, a half-cup of melted butter, a half-teaspoon of salt, and a dash of freshly grated nutmeg. Pour this mixture over the yams and carrots and bake it at 325° until it bubbles at the side. Once it cools, serve it with herbed pork tenderloin and crisp green beans. It's a meal any hungry soul would find refreshing after a hard day's work."

We followed printed recipes but our goal was to make these preparations a part of who we were. "When something good gets lodged in your head," she said, "it's there for life." This principle applies as much to conversion of heart as to food. Certain counsels become second nature to us—be they recipes for cooking or formulas for prayer. They are there when we sit at a finely set table, resplendent with good food, or when we need them to pave our way to the presence of God.

Main dishes in our home had to be the "feature attraction," a movie metaphor Mother liked to use. One such attraction was her batter-dipped fried flounder. It rivaled any fish and chips I tasted on my travels from London, England, to Sydney, Australia. Her batter consisted of one cup of flour, a half-teaspoon of baking powder, one egg, a half-teaspoon of salt with paprika, black pepper, diced parsley, and three-quarters of a cup of beer. Piece by piece we dipped the fish in the batter and then in seasoned breadcrumbs or cracker meal. We set the fillets in the refrigerator for an hour or so and then deep-fried them in hot vegetable oil. Served with homemade French fries, there was no end to our enjoyment of this dish.

We children customarily asked for seconds and thirds. Fourths were out of the question. That was when the rule of moderation had to be observed. The sauce we used was either homemade tartar or cocktail. Tartar called for a cup of mayonnaise, two-and-a-half teaspoons of relish, a tablespoon of chopped fresh parsley, one-and-a-half table-spoons of chopped onion, and a teaspoon each of Dijon mustard and horseradish. All of these ingredients were mixed together, chilled, and put in serving dishes to complement either batter-fried or broiled fish.

Cocktail sauce called for a half-cup of ketchup, a teaspoon of Dijon mustard, a teaspoon of chopped onions, three drops of Tabasco sauce, a teaspoon of vinegar and another of Worcestershire, and a dab of horseradish. Once stirred, it was ready to add zest to steamed or fried fish or jumbo shrimp—a treat on every holiday table.

Recalling such days and the good eating that accompanied them, I stand by my claim of the transformative power of heavenly food. It titillates my taste buds by virtue of memory alone. It elevates into imaginative recognition the colors, sights, smells, and sounds of the kitchen. Though gone physically, these sensations are there spiritually. Memory and imagination enkindle anticipation for the next time an old recipe is recreated. One awaits with bright-eyed hope the pleasure it continues to give grateful guests.

Food preparation and service are acts of love. No prepackaged frozen items, however energy-efficient and tasty they claim to be ("just like homemade"), can replace the exquisite experience of eating food prepared from scratch by a loving hand. Whether we said it aloud or merely thought the words, we knew, "It doesn't get any better than this."

A table full of hungry people, celebrating the spirit and the flavor of marvelous food, is a transformative event, exceeding, as do all transcendent experiences, our fondest expectations. In eyes rolling upward, in a symphony of little satisfied sounds, in the ear-to-ear smile of the cook when the dishes are done and the pots and pans are washed—all are witnesses in silent gratitude to the perfect wedding of body and soul.

Many meat dishes, like seafood specialties, conjure up a flood of sensations. Among the best are two preparations oft repeated, but never boring and always fulfilling. They are meatballs and pepper steak. Both became the perfect bait to keep friends coming to our kitchen to experience close encounters with unforgettable food.

Meatballs were as much a treat for us to make as they were for our guests to eat. Mother would start with two pounds of lean ground beef, preferably freshly ground round steak, deposited in a large mixing bowl. Then she added two cups of moistened, well-squeezed homemade or toast-ready white bread. To the meat and bread mixture, she cracked and folded in four eggs, a half-cup of imported Romano cheese, two teaspoons of salt, two teaspoons of pepper, a quarter-cup of chopped fresh parsley, a few finely chopped garlic cloves, a pinch of tiny fennel seeds, and a teaspoon of fresh or dry basil. Optional but "a good idea anyway" was to add three tablespoons of cream sherry and one teaspoon of garlic-infused olive oil.

Then, as if kneading bread, mother washed her hands, removed her rings, and began to work all the ingredients into the meat, squishing the mixture between her fingers until one item was blended into the other. Then her objective was to shape the meat mixture into small round, then slightly flattened balls and fry them in pure olive oil, keeping them tender but well done. After draining the meatballs on paper towels she sprinkled some more Romano cheese over them and served them to her guests, knowing that their mouths were already watering due to the aroma coming from the kitchen. The same meatballs, rolled a bit bigger, could be cooked in tomato sauce and served with spaghetti or, rolled a bit smaller, be put in wedding soup.

The mixture was versatile enough to be the basis of stuffed peppers, sweet and hot. She often would add to the basic meatball mixture a cup of finely ground carrots, a heaping tablespoon of mayonnaise, a dash of soy sauce, two tablespoons of ketchup, a half-cup of milk, and another heaping tablespoon of sour cream. Mixed together well, this became the "really special" stuffing for the peppers. She liked to broil and bag them, then remove their skin. That charred taste was delicious. Then she baked them for about forty minutes at 350° and once again we were the lucky recipients of a dish that always called for second helpings.

While Mother was not fixated on exact measurements, she was careful not to overdo any ingredients, especially condiments. Despite this lack of precision, whatever she prepared smacked of perfection. She cooked with spiritual verve. She gave everything her special touch. She had a good cook's best asset: intuition. She knew what went with what. This liberating approach kept the fun in home cooking and made of it an adventure worth repeating.

Mother's famous pepper steak (see recipe on page 123) had to be served on a warm homemade bun, "not mushy but with crunchy crust." The ingredients outlined here will serve two people, but they can be multiplied as needed. Sliver beef from a flank steak that has been seasoned and broiled. Julienne one red and one green pepper. Slice one Bermuda onion as thin as possible. Sliver two garlic cloves. Add a half-teaspoon of salt, some black pepper, and a tablespoon of Worcestershire sauce together in a small bowl. Then sauté all of these ingredients together and cook until tender. Sprinkle with a tablespoon of soft, sifted flour and add a half-cup of dry red wine. Cook a few more minutes until the mixture thickens a bit and serve hot and juicy on a fresh bun. With a side salad of diced tomatoes and fresh greens, this makes a wonderful lunch or a light dinner.

We inherited many "pass-it-on" recipes for chicken, but perhaps none was more memorable than Mother's cacciatore (see recipe on page 124). It was impossible to grow tired of this traditional Italian dish. As if she were still beside me I can hear her say: "Select three pounds of your favorite chicken pieces (breast, thigh, leg) and shake them in a bag where you've sifted flour, cornstarch, and seasonings like dried sage, rosemary, thyme, salt, and pepper." Then brown the chicken in a savory sesame seed oil. Remove it from the pan and add to the leftover oil a thinly sliced sweet onion, two cloves of crushed garlic, one cup of sliced mushrooms, a half-cup of diced yellow pepper, and some chopped basil and parsley. To these cooked vegetables add a large can of well-drained crushed tomatoes, a dash of oregano, and a half-cup of red wine. As the mixture begins to simmer, stir in one tablespoon of flour to thicken it. Then arrange the chicken in a large baking dish and add the vegetarian sauce to it. On top of everything spread a half-pound of separately sautéed buttery mushrooms with a few touches of roasted red peppers. Then spread over the entire casserole a cup of grated brick cheese. Heat everything in the oven for about thirty minutes and serve bubbling hot with a side of steamed broccoli.

Her favorite preparation for these was to trim a hearty bunch of the broccoli florets with a little of the stem left on them. She plunged the washed pieces into boiling water to cook but not overcook them. "They must stay green!" After draining them in a colander and running cold water over them, she put them in a basket-shaped serving bowl to show off their color. In a separate pan, she sautéed a chopped green pepper and some slivered garlic in olive oil. At the last minute she added some parsley and then poured this savory oil over the broccoli, sprinkling it with salt and pepper. She liked to serve this vegetable with a topping of Parmesan cheese and a squeeze of fresh lemon juice to bring out the flavor. Even broccoli-haters came to appreciate this dish!

Because it was rather expensive, we only had veal scaloppini once in a while, but, on those special occasions, it had to be prepared "à la Helen." She would beat two eggs in a bowl with a half-cup of cream, minced parsley, salt, pepper, and two ounces of grated Parmesan cheese. Then, after beating these basics well, she would add to them eight to ten thinly pounded veal scallops. Each would be pressed firmly in breadcrumbs and cooked golden brown in oil until they were tender—a few minutes on each side.

She would then transfer the cutlets to an ovenproof plate and place on each one a slice of prosciutto topped by one slice of imported provolone. In another pan she would bring to a boil a cup of beef bouillon and two tablespoons of red wine into which she added more parsley, a half-pound of sliced mushrooms, and a tablespoon of cornstarch diluted with some of the beef broth. Once the sauce was ready, she would pour it over the cutlets and place the dish for a few minutes under the broiler until the cheese melted and everything turned bubbly. It was utterly irresistible from the first to the last bite.

Dishes such as these satisfied hunger as well as the longing for harmony spiritually minded people seek. Being happy at the table is in its own way a religious experience, perhaps because it offers us a glimpse of the eternal happiness that can only be ours at the banquet table of the Lord.

Food for Thought

> O taste and see that the LORD is good;
>
> happy are those who take refuge in him. (Psalm 34:8)

In the annals of religious poetry, the metaphysical poet George Herbert (1593–1633) brings us to a table of heavenly plenty where Christ himself serves us as his guests, unworthy though we may feel of being the recipients of such an honor:

Love (III)

Love bade me welcome: yet my soul drew back,
  Guilty of dust and sin.
But quick-ey'd Love, observing me grow slack
  From my first entrance in,

Drew nearer to me, sweetly questioning,
If I lack'd anything.

A guest, I answer'd, worthy to be here:
Love said, You shall be he.
I the unkind, ungrateful? Ah my dear,
I cannot look on thee.
Love took my hand, and smiling did reply,
Who made the eyes but I?

Truth Lord, but I have marr'd them: let my shame
Go where it doth deserve.
And know you not, says Love, Who bore the blame?
My dear, then I will serve.
You must sit down, says Love, and taste my meat.
So I did sit and eat.[5]

Noticeable in "Love (III)" is the fact that love Divine welcomes us with open arms and insists that we are not strangers at this table. Though our spirit, heart, mind, and will might be scarred by sin and covered with the dust of unfulfilled desires, we still deserve the title Herbert gives us: "a guest worthy to be here."

Anyone who received an invitation to Mother's table knew they would be treated with the utmost respect. This atmosphere enabled them, if only for a little while, to rise above their troubles and talk of pleasant things. Cordiality prevailed over conflict. The love that went into the preparation of their meal made them feel loved in turn. If any item was not to their liking, the cook told them to set it aside and try another dish. Restless agitation subsided the minute the guests sat down. The tastes that awaited them were, according to their hostess, 100-percent deserved.

Thoughtful Food

Here is a recipe sure to please any palate. For it you will need four medium-sized washed portabella mushrooms; one cup of beef broth; two tablespoons of butter; four garlic cloves; and a half-teaspoon of sea salt. The process of preparation is simple, the result delicious.

Briefly sauté the mushrooms (stems removed) in melted butter and garlic. Turn over once or twice before pouring the beef broth over them. Sprinkle in the sea salt. Cover the pan and simmer the contents until the broth begins to reduce. Sprinkle the mushrooms with fresh parsley and freshly ground black pepper. Add a dash of sherry at serving time.

Be sure to add to the table a crusty Italian bread for soaking up the sauce. Side dish though this may be, it can be served as a first course, possibly followed by filet mignon and whipped red potatoes. This mushroom delight never failed to prompt someone to say: "Can you please give me the recipe?"

Another side dish features white mushrooms. Peel or brush (do not wash) one-and-a-half pounds of white mushrooms, remove the stems, and slice. Heat three tablespoons of butter in a large nonstick pan over medium heat, and add the sliced white mushrooms to it. Cook covered for five minutes, shaking occasionally. Then add two tablespoons of fresh lemon juice, sea salt, and black pepper to taste. Increase the heat, tossing the mushrooms well to mix. Add three teaspoons of crushed garlic, then toss and cook for two more minutes. Sprinkle in one tablespoon of chopped fresh parsley and heat the pan for one more minute, serving its savory contents immediately as a truly tasty side dish, complementing any meat or poultry you prefer.

Chapter Six
Final Touches

In the life of the spirit, there are as many unique souls in the process of being "transformed…from one degree of glory to another" (2 Corinthians 3:18) as there are foods emerging from an adventurous kitchen steeped in a love for creativity and tradition. Some souls may seem to be dry as flour dust or pliable as mashed potatoes, but all of them, like the diverse flavors on the table, must be treated with dignity and never taken for granted.

The food we prepare and consume with gusto ought to be fresh and full of surprises, never dull and drably routine. One day we need a soft touch, another a brisk knock. Is it possible that there could be an analogy between spiritual living and making piecrust? At times it comes out flaky and baked to perfection; at other times it is too tough, too loaded with shortening to digest, or simply too overworked. "Don't try too hard to make it happen," Mother reminded me. Learn to let go, to let be, and to live lightly.

When we made piecrust, the recipe that worked best consisted of three cups of sifted flour, a pinch of baking powder, a pinch of salt into which we cut one cup of Crisco and a half-cup of icy cold water. Once the ball of dough was formed, it could be rolled out and arranged in the pan to await a scrumptious filling, such as lemon meringue. To make it we mixed together one-and-a-half cups of sugar and three heaping tablespoons of cornstarch with a pinch of salt. We beat in three large egg yolks, reserving the whites for the meringue. Then we added one-and-a-half cups of water and a half-cup of fresh lemon juice with two teaspoons of lemon zest. We threw in a tablespoon of butter and a few drops of yellow food coloring and cooked the mixture, stirring constantly until it cooled and thickened. Then we poured it into an already baked, always flaky piecrust.

In a separate bowl we beat the three egg whites with one quarter-teaspoon of cream of tartar until they were thick and foamy. We continued beating and added one at a time six tablespoons of sugar and a half-teaspoon of vanilla. The key to meringue is not to under-beat it. Then we piled the meringue on top of the pie and baked it for ten minutes in a 350° oven until the topping was a delicate brown. We made sure to let the pie chill away from any draft so the peaks of meringue did not drop. Every tangy bite resulted in a lemony "pucker," the kind of smile a good pie brings to our lips.

Pecan pie was another family favorite. At holidays, such as the Fourth of July, Thanksgiving, and Christmas, we received shipments of these lovely nuts from our relatives in Alabama. We took a cup of pecan halves and arranged them in an unbaked pie shell—around the bottom in a circular configuration. Then we took three eggs and blended them with one cup of light corn syrup and a half-teaspoon of vanilla. Into that we added one tablespoon of melted butter. Then we combined one cup of sugar and one tablespoon of flour and blended that into the egg mixture, pouring all of it over the nuts already in the pie shell. Then we let it stand until the pecans rose to the top. That would enable them to glaze while baking. Forty-five minutes later, the pie emerged from the oven as if it were a ceramic masterpiece from a kiln.

Good cooks invent recipes on the spot and seldom write them on paper. Mother's recipe box held a lot of scraps on which she wrote cooking notes like "fast scratch cake," which consisted of two cups of sifted flour, a teaspoon of salt, a half-cup of sugar, and three teaspoons of baking powder, all placed in a mixing bowl. Beaten lightly together, in a separate bowl, were a half-cup of corn syrup, a quarter-cup of milk, and a half-cup of vegetable oil, to which she added two eggs, and a teaspoon each of vanilla- and orange-flavored syrup. She added a quarter-cup of freshly squeezed orange juice and some grated zest. That was beaten well into the flour mixture to which she added more flour as needed.

I rediscovered Mother's cooking philosophy on another note: "No fanatics belong near food. Loosen up; it will not hurt you. If something goes wrong, if it comes out tasting terrible, throw it away and learn from your mistakes. You'll do better next time. Trust me." She would bake the scratch cake batter in her favorite Bundt pan for about an hour at 325°. When the cake was done, she transferred it to a round dish and drizzled over it a few spoons of orange juice mixed with a quarter-cup of powdered sugar. She heated this mixture first, allowed it to cool, and then pricked the cake with a few fork holes so the juice flowed through it. The cake could be eaten as is or sliced thin to become the base for strawberry shortcake with fresh whipped cream. Sometimes she topped the cake with custard and peaches or whatever fruit was in season, knowing that not a scrap of it would be left on the plate.

The freedom I witnessed in her kitchen was to me the refreshing outcome of a solid spiritual life. It never hung so loose as to lose its moorings nor did it become so rigid as to cease knowing how to play and be creative. A kitchen in which cooks fail to laugh, sing, shout, and joke with one another may pass the test of serious cuisine but miss the more important test of a playful spirit. Food that is life-giving obviously comes from a lively kitchen.

The little cookies I'll next describe found their way into every celebration from baptisms to weddings to funerals. They were perfect complements to happy and sad occasions; they went well with laughter and tears. How they came to be began by mixing four eggs with a cup of vegetable oil and a half-cup of anisette liqueur. Then we added to this scented licorice mixture a half-cup of milk and four teaspoons of anise extract. We beat the ingredients well and added to them one-and-a-half cups of sugar into which we folded five cups of sifted flour and five teaspoons of baking power.

Mother noted with an experienced twinkle in her eyes, "the dough will be sticky, so you have to flour your hands and roll spoons of it into little balls." These were baked on a nonstick, lightly floured sheet for fifteen minutes at 350°. After they cooled we coated them with an icing made by mixing a cup of powdered sugar with some more anisette and a little milk. We dipped the top of each cookie in it, arranged them on a colorful platter, and expected them to be gone by the end of the evening.

Food like this never can be kept for one person or one family alone. It is meant to be shared. To be given the gift of food is to know how precious we are, both in the cook's and our Creator's eyes. These anise cookies were distributed to friends and strangers in gift boxes wrapped with seasonal paper and tied with a jaunty ribbon. They could be enjoyed with a cup of coffee or tea or offered as the perfect ending to dinner. They could even be eaten for breakfast with the beverage of one's choice.

This excursion into the transformative power of heavenly food proves that eating well is inseparable from the human longing for something more than mere relief of hunger. A person deprived of nourishment needs to fill up to live. No one would deny this basic need. Even so, this vital drive to survive, which has moved people to consume grass or bugs or tulip bulbs, tells us how resilient the human spirit is. Food is a commentary upon the ethnic group, the faith community, and the culture from which we emanate. Every town, village, city, state, and country has its own distinctive food, its special cuisine, its signature dishes. Whole cultures emerge around food: the Mediterranean, the German, the Lebanese, the Scandinavian, the Indian, the African, the Japanese, the Korean, the Thai, and the Vietnamese—the list is as endless as the demographics that make up the world.

People eat ordinary things like fruit and extraordinary things like alligator meat. Manners and etiquette surround eating customs, some using forks and knives, others sticks and fingers. Eating is ritualized and spiritualized. It calls for strict dietary laws and prohibitions, but it also encompasses cook-offs and food fights. People set world records by consuming everything from hot peppers to hot dogs. The Bible is full of ordinary and miraculous stories that focus on eating. Even the fall of the human race and its restoration is couched in an eating event (that infamous apple!).

From the consummation of forbidden fruit to the joy of Holy Communion, we cannot escape the effects of food on our whole being, for better or worse. We'll never know what course history might have taken had our first parents been content to dine on any other delicacy in the Garden of Eden than the one item prohibited by God. Happily for us, this fault had already been part of God's saving plan for them and us. When the Word became flesh and dwelt among us, he taught us through the witness of his disciples that we were not to "work for the food that perishes, but for the food that endures for eternal life, which the Son of Man will give you" (John 6:27).

Christ's followers challenged him with the story of how their ancestors had been fed manna in the desert. They got bread from heaven. What did Jesus have to offer? He told them in terms still unclear to their unbelieving ears that he was the true bread that comes down from heaven and "gives life to the world" (John 6:33). Naturally they wanted this bread for themselves but the mystery of what it meant was hard to swallow. Jesus made what must have sounded like an audacious claim: "I am the bread of life. Whoever comes to me will never be hungry" (John 6:35). This was good news, but it was also couched in a recipe hard to swallow. It would remain hidden from their eyes until the Feast of Pentecost when the Spirit of all truth would lift the veil from their minds and illumine their hearts. Only then could they pass the test of faith—a test based again on bread, for Jesus repeats in John 6:48, "I am the bread of life."

These "I am" statements of his are powerful and humble at the same time. He associates who he is with a commodity we eat practically every day. He knows that the memory of manna never left the narrative saga of the covenant people. It was a sign of their having been chosen by God to be a royal priesthood, a people set apart. Christ confirms the remembrance of what happened to their ancestors during their desert wanderings by reminding them that even though they had their fill of manna they still died. He offers them "the bread that comes down from heaven, which [they] may eat and not die," and then he identifies himself as the living bread that came down from heaven, announcing that anyone who eats of this bread will live forever (John 6:51).

This word went beyond any declaration they had ever heard. With inner ears open to his revelations, they received one more astonishing disclosure: "This bread is my flesh, which I give for the life of the world" (John 6:51). That set the room abuzz with every possible disputation.

Was he preaching cannibalistic behavior? Heaven forbid such blasphemy. Jesus held his ground. He made things worse by pressing on with his already outrageous claim: "I tell you the truth, unless you eat of the flesh of the Son of Man, and drink his blood, you have no life in you. Whoever eats my flesh and drinks my blood has eternal life, and I will raise [them] up at the last day" (John 6:54).

We must remember that all of these declarations were made by Christ prior to the Last Supper, Calvary, Easter Morning, the encounter on the road to Emmaus, and Pentecost itself. Here was a man, known to many as the son of a manual laborer in Nazareth, telling them in a calm, steady, unspectacular manner, "Those who eat my flesh and drink my blood abide in me, and I in them. Just as the living Father sent me, and I live because of the Father, so whoever eats me will live because of me" (John 6:56–57).

The eyes of his listeners must have bulged out of their sockets by then. They were incredulous. Jesus persisted. He repeated his point, however offensive they found it. He reminded them once more that their forefathers ate manna from heaven and still they died, but anyone who feeds on "this bread will live forever" (John 6:59). He had taught them many more lessons associated with food, such as eating corn on the Sabbath (Mark 2:23–24), but this teaching took place in an official setting, in the synagogue in Capernaum. No wonder many walked away from him that day.

Those words were too much for them to take, too life-changing in their implications. They were literally too much to swallow. Yet the Twelve did not leave him. Simon Peter explained why: "Lord, to whom shall we go? You have the words of eternal life" (John 6:68).

What a faith statement this friend, who later denied him, made at the very moment when Judas, the true betrayer, sought a way to denounce him to the Sanhedrin. He did so the night Jesus instituted the Eucharist in the room where he ate the Passover Supper with his disciples. The words were simple, but they changed the world, for he took bread, gave thanks, broke it, and passed it to them saying, "This is my body given for you" (Luke 22:17). Now, in the breaking of the bread, his saving task was revealed. Now they could take and eat this bread given to them for the life of the world.

The absolute generosity of God, depicted in the Scriptures, relies on food metaphors as a standard device. When God calls Ezekiel, he orders him to eat what is put before him, only instead of a piece of bread it is a whole scroll. God tells the prophet he has to eat this scroll if he is to speak to the house of Israel. So he opens his mouth and devours it. Then the Lord says to him: "Son of Man, eat this scroll I am giving you and fill your stomach with it." Ezekiel swallows everything! Then the text tells what happened next: "So I ate it, and it tasted as sweet as honey in my mouth" (Ezekiel 3:3).

To illustrate the abundance of God's graciousness to humankind, the Scriptures often refer to milk and honey, to flour, oil, and water. Prohibitions against foods that are unclean mark the formation of God's people just as acceptable foods like roasted lamb and unleavened bread mark their salvation. There are so many references to food in the Bible that it could be read as a divine cookbook filled with recipes for redemption. In the light of fatted calves and ripened figs, it would seem as if the "skin culture" represented by the Roman baths had to be replaced in the Judeo-Christian tradition by a "food culture."

Be that as it may, these eating metaphors are, if nothing else, wonderfully incarnational. Food set before a hungry body and a hungrier soul has about it an aura of saving grace. It connotes the banquet yet to come, not the dry taste of damnation. Imagine the horror the following prophecy (all food-oriented) must have made on the Egyptians to whom it was directed when Ezekiel bellowed out what the Sovereign Lord told him to say:

> I am against you,
>> Pharaoh king of Egypt,
> the great dragon sprawling
>> in the midst of its channels,
> saying, "My Nile is my own;
>> I made it for myself."
> I will put hooks in your jaws,
>> and make the fish of your channels stick to your scales.
> I will draw you up from your channels,
>> with all the fish of your channels
>> sticking to your scales.
> I will fling you into the wilderness,
>> you and all the fish of your channels;
> you shall fall in the open field,
>> and not be gathered and buried.
> To the animals of the earth and to the birds of the air
>> I have given you as food. (Ezekiel 29:3–5)

Such an unhappy fate is enough to make a body tremble and a soul turn in terror to God and beg for forgiveness. The king must repent in sackcloth and ashes. It would be better for him to eat dust than fall prey to wild beasts. It is so ironic that the early martyrs, who were thrown as food to the lions in the Colosseum of Rome, went to their death singing? What need was there for lamentations when they had found the bread of life?

The psalms etched on their hearts from ancient times reminded the Israelites of the heavenly banquet awaiting them, of fruit always in season (Psalm 1), of eternal pleasures (Psalm 16), of honey from the comb (Psalm 19). Their true destiny was to enjoy the heaven-sent delight of tasting and seeing the goodness of the Lord (Psalm 34). Better than any food from human hands would be this invitation to dine at the Lord's own table. By comparison, of what use was it to "eat the bread of wickedness and drink the wine of violence" (Proverbs 4:17)? Why would anyone choose this utterly indigestible diet and risk to boot the loss of body and soul? What might move such a hardened heart to select this recipe for unhappiness? Might its reversal necessitate nothing less than a visit by the Beloved himself, saying:

> A garden locked is my sister, my bride,
>   a garden locked, a fountain sealed.
> Your channel is an orchard of pomegranates
>   with all choicest fruits,
>   henna with nard,
> nard and saffron, calamus and cinnamon,
>   with all trees of frankincense,
> myrrh and aloes,
>   with all chief spices—
> a garden fountain, a well of living water,
>   and flowing streams from Lebanon. (Song of Songs
> 4:12–15)

Selfishness is the antithesis of divine generosity. Living in an egocentric circle of entrapment feels like eating a perpetually bad meal. The prophet Isaiah associates such selfishness with devouring every bush and beast in sight and still being hungry (Isaiah 9:20). Goodness is a wholly graced experience. It always gives us a full feeling; it is about never going hungry. Goodness brings us into the lush valley where the harvest is eternal and the vineyard forever in bloom, where we are surrounded by trees always yielding the ripest fruit, abundant and ready for picking. Souls who choose to be and do good, serving others for God's sake, receive abundant blessings. Their only wish is to pass them on to anyone in need of a crust of bread and a cup of water to go on with their search for holiness in the peaks and valleys of everyday life.

Food for Thought

No, "if your enemies are hungry, feed them; if they are thirsty, give them something to drink; for by doing this you will heap burning coals on their heads." Do not be overcome by evil, but overcome evil with good. (Romans 12:20–21)

The Bible reminds us again and again that the food on our table is meant to be shared with others, down to the crumbs that fall on the floor. Tables of love cut through traps of loneliness. Everyone is welcome there. Splendid feasts as well as pauper's fare—once shared—remind us of the wedding feast that God has prepared for those who love him. He tells us through the lips of the prophet Isaiah: "for I give water in the wilderness, rivers in the desert, to give drink to my chosen people, the people whom I formed for myself" (Isaiah 43:20–21).

The Most High God stoops to wait upon us. God can no more forget us than a mother could the baby at her breast (Isaiah 49:15). When the Lord comes to greet us, he lifts the veils covering our eyes and gives us a glimpse of the new heaven and the new earth. In the epicenter of this astonishing sight, we will see that "The wolf and the lamb shall feed together, / the lion shall eat straw like the ox; / but the serpent—its food shall be dust! / They shall not hurt or destroy / on all my holy mountain, / says the LORD" (Isaiah 65:25).

At the banquet of the Lord, justice has its day. The one who tempted Adam and Eve to eat forbidden fruit will be reduced to a diet of dust. Good overcomes evil. God's righteous anger gives way to a rushing stream of benevolent mercy. A virgin gives birth to the child destined to save us all. After the time of his teaching, when death exercises no power over him, he will rise on the third day. He will meet with his disciples by the lake, not with long-winded exhortations on his lips but with a simple invitation to enjoy the fish cooking on the fire and to come and have "breakfast with him" (John 21:12). Only when his followers are well fed, both physically and spiritually, will they be able to feed his lambs and tend his sheep (John 21:17) until that time when the Good Shepherd guides them to springs bubbling with the water of life and God wipes away every tear from their eyes (Revelation 7:17).

In the literature of spirituality there is a way to approach a text that has a food motif that makes it unforgettable. When we do spiritual reading says Guigo, a Carthusian, a monk of the twelfth century, we "imbibe" the sweetness of a blessed life.[6] He compares taking up a text to putting a ripe grape into your mouth. Now is the time to listen to the text with appreciation, humility, and attentiveness. In this way we may hear the slightest whispers of the Holy Spirit, who stirs our hearts and enlightens our minds.

Guigo describes meditation as "the busy application of the mind to seek with the help of one's own reason for knowledge of hidden truths." He says that meditation "perceives" the sweetness of God's benevolence. If reading puts food whole into the mouth, then meditation chews it or ruminates upon it, seeking the meaning of what God wants to convey to us. This reflection is not meant to be an extended exercise that relies on grappling with new information but an internal process of ruminating on the text at hand with the intention of going to the heart of its message.

If reading puts food into our mouth, if meditation chews it to assimilate its nourishing truths, then prayer extracts the flavor by means of praise, petition, intercession, and thanksgiving.

Contemplation occurs when "the mind is in some sort lifted up to God and held above itself, so that it tastes the joys of everlasting sweetness." It is as if God runs to meet the soul at prayer and to sprinkle the mind with "sweet heavenly dew." God restores the weary soul, slakes its thirst, and feeds its hunger.

To review, if reading ingests the food of God's Word, if meditation assimilates it, and if prayer extracts the flavor, then, as Guigo says, contemplation is the sweetness itself which gladdens and refreshes us like drinking a glass of fine wine in the company of cheerful friends and happy family members.

The result is that we enjoy the sweetness of divine contemplation not drop by drop, not now and then, but in an unceasing flow of delight that no one can take from us (John 16:22). We come to that place of unchanging serenity, marked by the peace and presence of God.

Thoughtful Food

There are two sauces a cook needs to master—one is a classic Italian meat sauce ideal with spaghetti and the other a splendid barbecue. Let's begin with my mother's classic preparation. You will need a large can of tomato puree and one can of Italian tomato paste, together with one small can of tomato juice. Have available one pound of ground pork and a half-pound of ground round steak.

In a large cooking pot, sauté in a half-cup of olive oil, three sliced garlic cloves, and one small chopped onion or two shallots. Then cook the ground beef and pork until they are thoroughly done. Pour the tomato puree into the pot. Dilute the paste with the tomato juice and add it next. Stir in some chopped fresh basil and parsley—about a quarter-cup each. Add salt and pepper, some red pepper flakes, and one teaspoon each of fennel seed and paprika. Stir well and bring to the boiling point. Then add two tablespoons of red wine and a half-cup each of Parmesan and Romano cheeses. Simmer for one hour, stirring occasionally. Serve over spaghetti prepared al dente—at least one pound for four people. Sprinkle with extra cheese if desired and bring piping hot to the table.

For a completely different occasion such as the Fourth of July, here is a barbecue sauce sure to please the palate of any connoisseur. Begin by mixing together a half-cup of vegetable broth with a tablespoon of brown sugar. Heat slowly and add two cups of diced onions, allowing them to caramelize. Then add one large can of crushed tomatoes followed by five cloves of crushed garlic. Stir to the boiling point over medium heat and add one-and-one-half cups of cider vinegar. Add salt and pepper to taste.

Simmer the sauce prepared so far for one hour. Then add to it a half-cup of honey, one tablespoon of Tabasco sauce, and one whole jalapeño pepper, diced and seeded. You may need to don a pair of gloves so the pepper does not burn your fingers. No, this secret sauce is not done yet! Add to it one can of tomato paste thoroughly incorporated into it. Cover the pot and simmer the sauce for forty to fifty minutes. Now take off the lid and add two tablespoons of all-natural "liquid smoke" flavoring. Taste the contents on the tip of a spoon to see if you need any more salt or pepper.

In the meantime you can put some chicken pieces (breast, wings, thighs) and some baby back ribs (two sections of six) in a roasting pan. Sprinkle them with salt and pepper and some all-purpose seasoning and roast well at 350°. Be sure the meat is cooked through. Then coat it liberally with the barbecue sauce. Return it to the oven to warm thoroughly. You are about to embark on a finger-licking-good meal dubbed by all as soul food!

Chapter Seven

Onward to Always-Memorable Meals

Physical sensations of hunger can be satisfied when we enjoy a fine meal. Our senses of sight and smell cause our mouths to water and ready us to eat our fill. It is not so easy to satisfy the hunger and thirst we feel as spiritual beings who long for even a brief encounter with the living God. What makes a meal most memorable is the combination of these two modes of being—physical and spiritual, provision for the body, providence for the soul.

Dissatisfaction occurs when we think that consumption of food, or, for that matter, of wealth or power or knowledge, will be enough to quell the deeper hunger of our spirit. Similarly, a disembodied approach to the spiritual life may make semi-starvation an end in itself, as if emaciation guarantees sanctification.

The appetite that God alone can satisfy has been implanted in us by Divine Mercy itself. It protects us from forfeiting what makes us human, which is nothing more or less than our capacity to taste and see that the Lord is good and that it is in him that we take refuge (see Psalm 34:8). Neither food nor drink taken in excess can fill that hole in our heart that longs for God. The Lord warns us not to let gluttony in any form usurp our quest for glory: "Be on guard so that your hearts are not weighed down with dissipation and drunkenness and the worries of this life, and that day catch you unexpectedly" (Luke 21:34).

In the life of glory, it is promised that we shall never again go hungry or feel as if we are dying of thirst. The Lamb himself will be our shepherd, leading us to the water of life (see Revelation 22:17). While this biblical truth may not always be uppermost in our minds, it is imperative that it sinks like essential nutrients into our hearts.

I have found from experience that keeping the balance between the physical and the spiritual is what makes a meal most memorable. My first thought when I prepare our family recipe for Three-Bean Chili is to anticipate that no one will leave the table feeling hungry. Theirs will be the happy satisfaction of stomachs full and spirits alight with the love of food for body and soul. From the assembling of the ingredients to the aroma of a simmering pot yielding a full dose of mouthwatering goodness, we are on the way to enjoying a memorable meal.

Have on hand two large center-cut pork chops; an eight-ounce can of chickpeas (garbanzo beans), along with the same portion of kidney beans and black beans, two small cans of Italian tomato sauce, one medium-sized red onion, two cloves of garlic, one green pepper, one red pepper, celery, carrots, and fennel seeds. You will also need fajita seasoning, cayenne pepper, cream sherry, and ketchup.

Preparation begins when you coat the pork chops lightly with olive oil. Season them with salt and pepper, and a teaspoon of fennel seeds, before roasting them in a 350° oven for about twenty-five minutes until they are almost cooked. Given the good aromas already filling the kitchen, someone is bound to drift in and ask, "What's cooking? It smells terrific." Anticipation is in the air. Spirits begin to soar. Provision and providence symbolize the bonding before God of body and soul.

In a nonstick soup pot, on a medium-high burner, sauté two table-spoons of olive oil, the three finely chopped garlic cloves, the diced red onion, the two slivered celery stalks, and the carrots, stirring until lightly cooked. Add the green and red pepper, both chopped, and lower the heat a notch.

Drain the chickpeas, kidney beans, and black beans, and add them to the pot. Season with black pepper, one half-teaspoon of cayenne pepper, a tablespoon of parsley flakes, and a teaspoon of fennel seeds, and, of course, fajita seasoning to taste. Next add the two cans of tomato sauce, one quarter-cup of ketchup, and the same amount of cream sherry.

Everything comes together in this symphony of Three-Bean Chili. The excitement builds for the cook and those continually coming into the kitchen with senses attuned to the process—seeing, smelling, and hearing the music of a bubbling pot, touching shoulders with affection, and begging for a little taste—but not yet. The secret to success with this dish comes next. Remove the almost-cooked pork chops from the oven and cool them enough to cut them into bite-sized pieces. Drop them into your chili pot and give everything a stir. Allow this little masterpiece to simmer covered for approximately forty-five minutes to an hour. Serve in colorful bowls with corn bread on the side.

What makes a meal memorable might be something as simple as penne with fresh pesto sauce. Combine in a food processor or blender for one or two minutes a half-cup of pine nuts (pignoli), two cups of fresh basil leaves, two cloves of garlic, and a half-cup of extra virgin olive oil. Add two-thirds cup of freshly grated Parmesan cheese and a teaspoon of salt with ground black pepper to taste. Set aside while you cook one pound of penne. Drain, reserving one cup of the pasta water, then put the pasta into a serving bowl and drizzle with a few tablespoons of melted butter or olive oil. Mix the pasta water with the pesto, and pour over the penne, blending together. Sprinkle with more Parmesan cheese and serve with crusty Italian bread and chilled white wine. Compliments to the chef!

Small meals like this have about them the aura of a banquet to be enjoyed by few or many. Status symbols shrink in importance. Everyone enjoys the same fare and no one feels cheated. This dish is a welcome sight on a weekday night as well as a birthday or anniversary celebration. Food like this celebrates human equality and dignity. Both paupers and princes enjoy it. No wonder Jesus welcomes sinners to his table and dines with them (Luke 15:1–2).

At the table of plenty there is no sign of decadence or defeat, doom or gloom. Appreciative exchanges grace the table and everyone feels better than when they sat down. Years later they may recount such pleasant times together: "I'll never forget how quickly that pasta disappeared. We dipped our bread in fragrant olive oil. We drank a few glasses of wine. We talked about everything under the sun. It's a moment I'll never forget." Is it too bold to predict that heaven may be a little bit like this, a festive feast, with music and dancing and really good food through which God reveals his faithfulness to us? The fruits of covenant love abound, just as the prophet Isaiah predicted:

> On this mountain the LORD of hosts will make for all peoples
> a feast of rich food, a feast of well-aged wines,
>   of rich food filled with marrow, of well-aged wines strained
>   clear.
> And he will destroy on this mountain
>   the shroud that is cast over all peoples,

the sheet that is spread over all nations;

he will swallow up death forever.

Then the Lord GOD will wipe away the tears from all faces,

and the disgrace of his people he will take away from all the
earth,

for the LORD has spoken. (Isaiah 25:6–8)

Food for Thought

They will hunger no more, and thirst no more; / the sun will
not strike them, / nor any scorching heat; / for the Lamb at
the center of the throne will be their shepherd, / and he will
guide them to springs of the water of life, / and God will wipe
away every tear from their eyes. (Revelation 7:16–17)

Just as in every end we find a new beginning, so, too, when one meal
comes to a happy conclusion cooks are already planning the next. Food
is not an option. We must nourish ourselves or else risk disease and
death by starvation. Food sources display a variety that boggles the
mind. What is a delicacy for some people horrifies others. A neighbor
across the ocean in Africa may relish eating ants while his or her coun-
terpart on the continent finds truffles a treasure to the sophisticated
palate. In a prison camp stale bread becomes a coveted provision. On
a street in Paris bakery outdoes bakery in producing masterpieces of
pastry.

I like to think of food as one of God's greatest gifts, as basic as the air
we breathe and the water we drink. Food is at creation's door, for in the
Garden of Eden God gave our first parents access to the fruits found on
every seed-bearing tree. The forbidden fruit, once consumed, caused a
disastrous split between us and God but apples as such are so good that
one a day may really keep the doctor away!

All living creatures need to find something to eat. In the circle of life there is a dance of dining unfolding day and night. All find their proper food in every season, and for that provision we must give thanks. Feast ebbs and famine flows, and the life cycle presses toward celebration and sheer survival. Chosen ones like the prophet Elijah count on God to give them what they need to complete their mission. He was not disappointed. There was for him water from a brook and bread and meat brought by birds in the morning and evening (1 Kings 17:1).

Obedient servants are not surprised to see that the Lord serves them. Food for man and beast is never bland. Think of how pleasurable is the flavor of one piece of fine chocolate, how lovely the texture of a garlic-crusted bread stick. Do we not relish the color of a bowl of ripe strawberries, the shape of a cheese ball, the smell of hot cider on a snowy evening?

Such food is a pointer to the miracle of creation and the sheer creativity of our Creator. Here is a biblical bowl of fruit: figs (Deuteronomy 8:8); apples (Proverbs 25:11); grapes (Matthew 7:16); raisins (1 Samuel 25:18); and that is just a start. The first miracle Jesus performed was to turn water to wine (John 2:11). He spoke of pinches of salt and measures of yeast. He walked through a homeland flowing with milk and honey (Exodus 3:8). He made sure that we understand the difference between animal sacrifice and total reliance on the mercy of God. He compared himself to a lamb whose sacrifice on the cross was our only hope of salvation.

Food is to be shared, not to be hoarded in barns where it rots away. God's providence offers enough for all. That is why hunger ought to be eradicated as much as possible from the earth. After all, over this provision we are to behave as stewards, not possessors. Otherwise God has no choice but to fill the hungry with good things and to send the rich away empty (Luke 1:53).

Consider in conclusion that God gives us not only food for the body but a constant stream of food for the soul. Grace knows no bounds. We who "eat" the words of the Lord do not need to worry about what to eat at table today or tomorrow. Spiritually, we know and believe with every fiber of our being that "life is more than food, and the body more than clothing" (Luke 12:23). This orientation to the transcendent is what makes us distinctively human, alike in some ways but radically different from any other form of life on earth.

While striving to put food for body and soul on the table, we seek on a higher plane to make the reign of God a reality on earth. We are disciples of a generous Master whose "food" was "to do the will of [the Father]" who sent him to finish his work (John 4:34). That work must also become our highest goal and our purpose for being on earth. We are not merely consumers but communicators of the Good News. We do not work for food that spoils but for that which endures to eternal life (John 6:27). We thank the Lord for working miracles in the area of physical food—from manna to the multiplication of the loaves and fishes—but we would be nothing were it not for the fact that he gave us the bread of life, which never grows stale. Each day becomes a new one for us because the bread we eat is his Body and the wine we drink eucharistically is his Blood.

On this spiritual plane fear of starvation subsides because we who believe in him will never go hungry and we will never be thirsty (John 6:35), for, as he says, "my flesh is real food and my blood is real drink" (John 6:55). Difficult as this teaching is, it does not occur to us to turn away, since the Lord of life himself is our teacher. We can only imagine what it must have been like to witness that Passover feast in the Upper Room when he celebrated that first Eucharist in the breaking of the bread.

Knowing the customs of the time, we cannot doubt that the disciples were treated physically to a sumptuous meal. At a moment resplendent with heavenly light, their taste transcended the banquet table fare and soared to a heavenly place that was about to transform every meal anyone might eat on earth. The Lord of glory gave them and us his very self, saying, "This is my body" (Matthew 26:26) and, "This is my blood," the blood of the covenant, "poured out for us for the forgiveness of sins" (Matthew 26:28). No meal can match this promise. Every morsel we eat becomes a sacrament of thanksgiving, pointing to the food that nourishes our soul, welling up inside of us like a spring of water gushing up to eternal life" (John 4:14).

Thoughtful Food

It seems fitting that we not forget dessert and the best recipe I can offer in a book devoted to food that pleases all our senses is my own for carrot cake. The ingredients required for its creation are as follows:

- 2½ cups walnut halves
- 1¼ cups sifted all-purpose flour
- 1 teaspoon salt
- ½ teaspoon nutmeg
- ½ teaspoon cinnamon
- 1 teaspoon baking soda
- 1 teaspoon baking power
- 3 eggs
- 1 teaspoon vanilla
- 1 cup of granulated sugar
- ¾ cup vegetable oil
- ¼ cup orange liqueur (Grand Marnier, for example)
- 1 teaspoon orange marmalade

- 3 cups grated carrots
- 1½ cups raisins

Now what? First drop the walnuts into boiling water for five minutes. Drain them well and spread them in a shallow baking pan. Toast them at 350° for fifteen to twenty minutes, until they are golden brown. Shake them off and on so they do not burn. Set aside a half-cup of nuts for decorating the cake when it's done. Chop the remainder coarsely.

In a large bowl, resift the flour with the salt, baking soda, and powder. Beat the eggs and fold in the sugar, oil, orange liqueur, and marmalade. Add this to the flour mixture and beat into a smooth batter. Stir in the carrots, raisins, and chopped walnuts. Turn into a greased and floured ten-inch round tube pan and set it in the oven or on a sheet of aluminum foil. Bake at 350° for one hour or until the cake tests done with a toothpick. Cool in the pan and then remove it to a serving dish. Spread it with cream cheese frosting and decorate it with the walnut halves.

For the frosting, cream together six ounces of cream cheese (room temperature) with a half-cup of softened butter. Add a teaspoon of orange liqueur (same brand as in the cake). Gradually beat in three cups of sifted confectioner's sugar. Generously spread on your cake and be prepared to enjoy every morsel.

Afterword

Writing this book has given me a clearer view of the connection between the food we consume for physical survival and the meditations on life that let us thrive as spiritual beings. Eating ought not to be an end in itself, like fueling our cars, but a means to celebrate the spirit/mind/body unity we are. Food, being essential for our survival, is a commodity we cannot live without.

In my family of origin, as this book has shown, the one unarguable goal was to put good food for body and soul on the table. For that reason alone, whatever the weather, with or without a home repair contract in his pocket, my hard-working father got up every morning, dressed in overalls or a suit and tie, and hit the pavement. Undernourished children, starting with myself and my two brothers, were not an option for him. Our early life was table-centered and for that I will be forever grateful.

Food is as essential to our existence as milk and motherhood are lifelines to an infant. The cry for sustenance arises from the baby's little soul. It is the cry that makes us weep when we see the shriveled torso of a starving child deprived of food and, as a consequence, lacking the energy that comes with regular intakes of nutrition.

The marvel of our body's digestive system suffers great setbacks due to undernourishment. Think of it. This system takes in "fuel" in the form of food, "processes it, and sends it to the cells, where biochemical processes convert it into usable fuel for the tiny cellular bodies."[7] This complex system involves many organs (liver, stomach, spleen, kidneys) and a multitude of chemicals and enzymes.

Gastric fluids such as hydrochloric acid, in just the right concentration, nourish us without causing tissue damage. Digestion is a fascinating process. We eat a luscious bite of food oblivious to what our body does with it. All we know is that we are happy souls, clicking our forks, slicing and dicing with our knives, sipping wine and toasting our guests. A world of structural and neurochemical forces are set in motion while we serenely finish our meal.

Dr. Richard A. Swenson becomes almost poetic when he speaks of our three-pound liver which, next to the skin, is the largest organ of the body. Its three hundred billion cells perform over five hundred functions, yet when was the last time we were in awe of our own liver?

All of the blood flowing away from the stomach and intestines must first pass through the liver before reaching the rest of the body. The liver is thus situated at a crucial crossroads, entailing countless responsibilities. It detoxifies substances, guards vitamin and mineral supplies, stockpiles sugar, produces quick energy, manufactures new proteins, regulates clotting factors, controls cholesterol, makes bile, maintains hormone balance, stores iron, assists immune function, and is even responsible for making the fetal blood cells in the womb. One thing it does not do is complain. It will work and work without protest, even under enormous abuse.[8]

Little wonder, for a person without a functioning liver, despite this organ's amazing regenerative potencies, the only thing that stands between his or her life or death is a transplant. What strikes Dr. Swenson as especially remarkable is the fact that irresponsible eating on our part—rooted in a dualistic split between body and soul, oblivious to the fact that we are what we eat—does not immediately destroy the design of our body on God's part.

It takes an enormous expanse of bad and unhealthy decisions to erode or destroy the fearful and wonderful creatures we are. In these wise words of C.S. Lewis, cited by Swenson, "[God] himself is the fuel our spirits were designed to burn, or the food our spirits were designed to feed on. There is no other. That is why it is just no good asking God to make us happy in our own way without bothering about religion. God cannot give us happiness and peace apart from himself, because it is not there. There is no such thing."[9]

Just as the food of Jesus was ultimately to do the will of the Father who sent him to save us, so we need to appreciate the truth that our very bodies are the temple of God. It is our duty to do all that we can to maintain them—from practicing table etiquette versus gross consumption to preparing nutritious meals so easily digestible that they never cause bloating. In this way we respect God's precious and brilliant bodily design, revealing an exquisite balance consisting of three-fourths water and just the right amount of fat from the moment he knit us together in our mother's womb (Psalm 139).

Temple maintenance (since we are temples of the Holy Spirit) is a spiritual exercise. Complementing the customary disciplines of reading, meditation, and prayer are those of diet, exercise, and sleep. In both cases, we respect the creative power and precision of God beheld not only in the far reaches of the cosmos but when we pause to look at ourselves in a mirror.

When a meal lovingly prepared and served is good to the last drop we do taste a bit of heaven on earth. There are certain meals etched in our memories that convince us that nothing could be better. Never will I forget breakfast in a Spanish inn overlooking the city of Granada radiant in the morning sun. The eggs were perfectly prepared, with beautiful reddish-yellow centers, fresh as the free-range chickens in the courtyard below could lay them. The freshly toasted bread crisped in olive oil was made for dipping. The richly fragrant hot coffee with thick cream was worth every sip. Fresh fruit—from figs to blood red oranges to toasted walnuts—made of the morning meal a perfect start to the journey that lay ahead. It is almost as if I can still taste that breakfast and the upsurge of thanks I felt for it. Great is the Lord and greatly to be praised.

At moments like this we know that we are more than a "random collection of organized items." As Swenson concludes, "Within the miracle of the human body, there is sanctity, hope, and glory. More important, this same awareness also helps us to appreciate that such a Creator is rightly regarded with awe."[10]

As Scripture tells us, our body is to become nothing less than a living sacrifice, holy and pleasing to God, whose only Son became one of us in the flesh in all things but sin. The incarnation is the greatest testimony to the union of body and soul. Christ Jesus ate, drank, and slept, as we must do every day. He reclined at table, enjoyed breaking bread with friends, took care of his private needs, bathed, dressed, and walked most of the time to keep fit. He grew in wisdom and grace, from babyhood to adulthood, showing us how to live and, in the end, how to die.

We could say that he lived a spiritually organic life as simple as it was profound.

Just as he put himself and each of us in a body, so he put that body into membership with his Body where everything works in unison with a purpose whose perfect design will only be revealed to us in the life to come where eye has not seen nor ear heard what God has in store for those who love him (1 Corinthians 2:9).

For now, begin to look at your body and your soul with wonder. With every morsel you eat, do not presume to understand the mystery that you are. Instead be in awe of each moment of life that courses through your veins, of each breath you inhale and exhale. What wondrous God is this who can package together trillions of atoms, greater than the number of stars in the universe; billions of subatomic particles; sixty million gallons of blood coursing through sixty thousand miles of blood vessels; to say nothing of a three-pound brain that contains ten billion neurons and growing, and has one hundred trillion neurological interconnections. These are only a few of the bodily statistics presented by Swenson, but they are enough to arouse wonder and gratitude as we glimpse but a fraction of what it means to be made in the form and likeness of God.

Let me conclude this excursion into a spirituality of food for body and spirit by suggesting a practical, seven-step program that, with the help of grace, may lead to a more balanced approach not only to cooking and eating but also to a spiritually renewed life that tastes and sees at every moment the goodness of the Lord

1. Seeing Simply

Try to see everyday things like utensils, pots and pans, and ingredients leading to a splendid table as pointers to the transcendent. Move beyond their surface meaning to the hidden light of truth embedded in them. Let go of frantic functionalism long enough to enjoy a good meal. With a slight change of attitude, you can begin to see daily life as an epiphany of God's presence. The standard for transformation is not seeing a direction and taking it but following God's guiding hand wherever it points. My futile effort to attain perfection, for example, when preparing a meal for prestigious guests, gives way to gentle attempts to do the best I can and not to worry if one chicken bone shows up in the soup.

Seeing simply causes surface seeing to recede. Depth vision takes its place. I behold the giftedness of all that is. Worldly clutter and complexity give way to a rediscovery of the simple. Mine becomes an eye trained to catch the splendor of everything around me from a leaf of lettuce to a banquet fit for a king. Now I see the invisible good behind every visible gift.

2. Listening Attentively

Proper listening, for example, to a master chef sharing a few secrets, frees me from distractions. Instead of straining to grasp every detail, I attend to the few points I do understand, knowing that knowledge will grow with experience.

To listen at this depth presupposes the practice of inner stilling. It places me in a posture of readiness to receive what I am able to hear and to refrain from jumping to conclusions.

Attentive listening assures me that there is more to this message than a first hearing of it reveals. I need to digest and assimilate with patience and perseverance new ideas based on tried-and-true kitchen experiences. Listening attentively to the wise directives of reputable cooks puts me in an ideal position to practice what they teach. Docility makes me a teachable disciple who may one day become a master of the culinary arts.

3. Dwelling Repeatedly

I cannot expect to see or hear instantly what these exercises in practical spirituality open to my view unless I am willing to dwell repeatedly on them. It may take many starts to come to the good ending of a meal. Then it feels as if I have returned to homeport after explorations on hitherto unknown seas. Repetition enables the pursuit of excellence in the kitchen or anywhere else. It provides a point of reference, a learning tool, on the way to the goals I have set for myself under the inspiration of the Spirit. Repeated attempts to execute a recipe are not a matter of blind conformity to the text but of trying to appropriate the basics so I can creatively embellish them.

Dwelling repeatedly invites me to make a new discovery each time I cook for myself or others. I cannot predict where this respectful approach may lead, but I am willing to seek modes of improvement rather than settle for mediocrity. A mistake made here or there is not a source of frustration but an invitation to return again to what intrigues me. Only then does the door of insight open a little more. I cease strenuous attempts to master my art and begin to appreciate the way in which the food I prepare happens to taste delicious when I least expect it. Good cooking is and remains a mystery. Every start is a new opportunity to realize my potential. Thanks to repeated dwelling, my meal preparation is less likely to meander from one recipe to another. I become more focused, less frustrated. I stop repeatedly not only to assess my direction but to seek nourishment from the wellsprings of spiritual living.

4. Waiting Patiently

I must not push the cooking process impatiently. Otherwise I risk losing peace of mind and joyful presence. I clog the channels of seeing simply, listening attentively, and dwelling repeatedly already opened to me. I let go of shoulds and oughts, musts and nevers. I stay away from the fast-track of living in restaurant chains and allow myself the luxury of slowing down to enjoy a home-cooked meal.

Such waiting requires that I let go of junk food and remain committed to the "joy of cooking," which was Julia Child's favorite phrase. I relax my anxious striving to please ultimately unpleasable people and trust my intuition of what tastes good to common folks like myself. I may not follow someone else's recipe to a T, but in the long run I find the way that is best for me.

Waiting patiently is a matter of receiving and responding to the challenging, inviting, and appealing gift that life is. To wait upon the splendor of the ordinary at table and elsewhere is to wait for the gift of maturing in wisdom and grace—a sure sign that I may be dubbed one day a hostess with the mostest!

5. Practicing the Right Rhythm of Trying and Succeeding

Good cooking calls for the avoidance of extremes. Too much effort executed under the pressure of perfectionism can lead to the kind of frustration that escalates fear of failure and smothers initiative. Too much success may lead to the opposite attitude—an arrogant kind of complacency and narcissistic assurance that mocks any attempt to prepare a less-than-perfect dish. One risks becoming puffed up with one's own importance accompanied by remarks that may be unkind, curt, discourteous, and impatient.

Balance is not easy to attain because it entails finding the middle way, neither setting impossible standards of success nor giving up too quickly. To avoid either extreme, I need to assess the situation in which I find myself (are my guests coming for lunch or dinner?), regain the proper perspective, and do what I can to make the meal a happy occasion for everyone.

6. Balancing Eating Alone and Dining with Others

It is a source of concern to find that a slipshod approach begins to be acceptable when one has to eat alone. The worst "sin" of singleness is, in my opinion, opening a can of tuna fish or making a peanut butter and jelly sandwich and calling it dinner. Aloneness at the table ought to command as much respect as togetherness. Solitude with the Lord as one's companion is to be celebrated as much as solidarity with others. Neglect of either side of our call—its uniqueness or its commonality— may lead to a highly imbalanced life. Look at it this way: My uniqueness becomes a pointer to universal needs. Separateness heightens my attention to what we have in common. Aloneness increases the sense of my oneness in relation to all that is.

7. Following the Ebb and Flow of Giving and Receiving

Life discloses itself as an ebb and flow between giving (of my support, talents, time) and receiving (of another's hospitality, care, and friendship). Growth in spiritual maturity is inconceivable without this rhythm of donation and reception.

Goodness received and given offers me an abundance of chances for personal and spiritual enrichment. Giving care enables me in noticed and unnoticed ways to express my love for others. Receiving care reminds me that life itself comes to us freely in all its beauty. We cannot schedule its delivery, but we can stand in readiness to receive it.

A lesson I have learned from cultivating a spirituality of food for body and soul merits repeating: The more I live in love, the more those I serve announce with every bite they take a deeper appreciation of themselves and others—a philosophy of life recorded in this closing prayer:

Lord, allow me to enjoy unstressed this moment of rest,
this time of grace around the table of plenty you and I have

prepared. Thank you for this food and for all it means to me and my guests. Lord, your grace is never wanting. May it always be outpoured to hungry people like us, longing to be fed in body and spirit. Amen.

Recipes

Here are the recipes for many of the dishes discussed in this book.

Eggplant Parmagiana

- 3 medium-sized eggplants
- 1 cup flour
- 2 tablespoons cornstarch
- 1 teaspoon each black pepper, oregano, and paprika
- ¼ cup cream
- 5 eggs
- 2 tablespoons fresh basil (or 2 teaspoons dried)
- 2 tablespoons fresh parsley (or 2 teaspoons dried)
- 1 teaspoon chives
- 2 tablespoons cream sherry (e.g., Harvey's Bristol Cream)
- 2 tablespoons olive oil
- 2 cups tomato sauce; see recipe below to make your own, or use a 16-ounce jar of sauce
- 1 cup grated Parmesan cheese

Peel the eggplant and cut it into slices one-quarter-inch thick, salt generously, and let stand for an hour. In the meantime, use a shallow bowl or plate big enough for dipping, and make a dry rub consisting of the flour, 1 tablespoon cornstarch, and a seasoning of black pepper, oregano, and paprika. In another shallow dish mix 1 tablespoon cornstarch, along with the cream, eggs, salt and pepper, basil, parsley, chives and the cream sherry.

Rinse the eggplant slices in cold water, and squeeze them gently to remove the excess. Put each of the slices, one at a time, in the dry rub, then in the batter, then lay them on a large plate. When all the slices have been coated, set a large skillet coated with olive oil on the top of the stove, and gently heat it. Place the eggplant in the pan, one layer at a time. Cook on one side for 3 minutes, then turn and brown the other side for 3 minutes. As each batch of eggplant slices is browned, lay it on a platter atop paper towels to absorb any excess oil. Continue to fry the slices, adding oil to the pan as needed.

Coat the bottom of a casserole pan with tomato sauce. Arrange the browned slices of eggplant in a flat casserole pan alternating them with tomato sauce and a generous helping of grated Parmesan cheese. You should have 2 or 3 layers of eggplant when done. Place the casserole in a 325° oven to bake for an hour.

When cooking is complete, let the dish sit for about twenty minutes before serving.

Tomato Sauce
for Eggplant Parmigiana

- 2 cloves garlic
- 2 tablespoons olive oil
- 1 small onion
- 1 small green pepper

- 1 small red pepper
- 28-ounce can crushed tomatoes
- 4-ounce can tomato paste
- ½ cup vegetable broth
- ¼ cup Marsala wine
- 2 tablespoons fresh parsley (or 1 teaspoon dried)
- 2 tablespoons fresh basil (or 1 teaspoon dried)
- Salt and pepper

Slice the garlic, and dice the onion and peppers, then sauté them together in a pan for 5 minutes. Pour the mixture into a deep pot with a lid, and add the crushed tomatoes, tomato paste, and vegetable broth. When the sauce comes to a boil add the Marsala wine, parsley, and basil. Salt and pepper to taste. You can add a teaspoon or so of red pepper flakes if you'd like some extra zing in the sauce. Let simmer over medium-low heat, covered, for 90 minutes.

Marinated Mushrooms

- 1 pound white button mushrooms
- 1 cup dry white wine
- ⅓ cup olive oil
- 1½ teaspoons salt
- ½ teaspoon black pepper
- ½ teaspoon oregano
- 2 tablespoons chopped parsley
- 2 tablespoons diced white onion
- 1 large clove garlic, minced
- 3 tablespoons fresh lemon juice

- ½ cup white vinegar
- 1 bay leaf
- 1 teaspoon dill
- 1 tablespoon sugar
- 1-quart Mason jar

Wash and slice the mushrooms and put them in the Mason jar. Combine the rest of the ingredients in a stainless-steel pan and simmer for 15 minutes (the mixture must not boil, only simmer). Pour the mixture over the mushrooms and let the jar cool down for about a half hour. Put the jar in the refrigerator for 3 to 4 hours. The mushrooms are then ready to eat. They can be kept in the refrigerator after opening for up to two weeks.

Pickled Eggplant

- 1-quart Mason jar
- 1 eggplant
- ½ cup white vinegar
- 2 to 3 garlic cloves
- 1 teaspoon salt
- 1 to 2 sliced hot peppers
- ½ cup olive oil

Peel the eggplant and cut into cubes, then pack into the Mason jar. Add the remaining ingredients, then cover the jar tightly. Shake the contents several times to blend the ingredients, and put the jar in the refrigerator. Chill overnight, then use as a garnish. Eggplant will keep in the refrigerator after opening for up to two weeks.

Eggplant Bruschetta

- 2 medium eggplants
- 1 cup chopped celery
- 8-ounce can plum tomatoes, diced (or use 1 cup fresh tomatoes that have been blanched and peeled, then diced)
- 1 red pepper, diced
- 1 shallot, sliced thin
- ½ cup black olives
- ¼ cup capers
- Salt and pepper
- 1 cup mushrooms, any variety, sliced
- 2 to 3 garlic cloves, minced
- 2 tablespoons olive oil
- 2 to 3 sprigs fresh parsley, chopped without stems
- 1 teaspoon red pepper flakes (optional)

Peel and cube the eggplants, and discard the seeds. Sprinkle salt over the cubes and mix well, then let the eggplant sit for an hour. Rinse and drain the cubes, then put them in a bowl. Add the chopped celery, diced tomatoes, red bell pepper, shallot, black olives, and capers. Mix everything together, adding salt and fresh ground pepper to taste. Sauté the sliced mushrooms in olive oil with the garlic cloves for about 5 minutes. Add the mushrooms to the eggplant mixture, along with the parsley and red pepper flakes. Mix together. Serve on crackers or toasted bread slices.

Chopped Chicken Livers

- 2 pounds fresh chicken livers
- 2 tablespoons olive oil
- 1 tablespoon butter
- 1 teaspoon salt
- ¼ teaspoon black pepper
- ¼ teaspoon paprika
- 2 tablespoons chicken broth
- ½ teaspoon dried sage
- 2 tablespoons chopped onion
- 3 sprigs fresh parsley, chopped with no stems
- 1 tablespoon basil
- 1 shallot, sliced thin
- 1 clove garlic
- ¼ cup cream sherry (e.g., Harvey's Bristol Cream)
- Dash of Worcestershire sauce
- ¼ cup chopped celery
- ½ teaspoon Dijon mustard
- 1 tablespoon mayonnaise
- 4 hard-boiled eggs, chopped finely

Begin by boiling the eggs for 10 minutes; set aside to cool when done. Rinse the chicken livers and pat dry, then sauté them in 1 tablespoon of the olive oil and the butter for 5 minutes, turning the livers so they brown evenly. Add the salt, black pepper, paprika, chicken broth, the remaining olive oil, sage, chopped onion, parsley, basil, shallot, and garlic. Mix together, and sauté for a few minutes longer, until the liquid has cooked down. Blend the remaining ingredients into this thickened mixture.

Put the chicken liver mixture into the bowl of a food processor, and pulse until coarsely chopped, about 6 to 8 times (do not puree). Serve on Melba toasts, crisp wheat crackers, or matzo.

Meatloaf

- 2 pounds lean ground beef
- 1 cup bread cut into cubes, then dampened and squeezed dry
- 1 cup mashed potatoes
- 1 cup ricotta cheese
- 4 eggs
- ½ cup heavy cream
- ½ cup mayonnaise
- ¼ cup ketchup
- 1 teaspoon cornstarch
- ¼ cup Marsala wine
- Dash of Worcestershire sauce
- Salt and pepper to taste

Place the meat in a large mixing bowl, and add the bread cubes, mashed potatoes, ricotta, heavy cream, mayonnaise, and ketchup. Knead the whole mixture by hand until all the ingredients are blended. Season to taste with salt and pepper, and a few drops of Worcestershire sauce. Shape into a loaf and place in a nonstick shallow pan; bake at 350° for one hour.

When the meatloaf is done, remove from pan and wrap in aluminum foil; set aside. Put the drippings from the meatloaf pan into a small saucepan over low heat. Add the cornstarch and Marsala wine, then thicken slowly, for 5 to 10 minutes. Unwrap the meatloaf and drizzle the sauce over it, then serve.

Mother's Bread

- 6½ cups bread flour
- 2 (.25 oz.) packages active dry yeast
- 3 tablespoons white sugar
- 2½ cups warm water
- 3 tablespoons shortening (e.g., melted butter or Crisco)
- 1 tablespoon salt

In a large mixing bowl, dissolve yeast, sugar, and ½ cup of the warm water. Let sit for a few minutes until yeast gets foamy. Add shortening, salt, and 2 cups flour to yeast mixture, and stir together with a large spoon. Then add the remaining flour to the mixture, 1 cup at a time, blending with the spoon or your hands. When all the ingredients have been mixed together, turn the dough onto a wooden cutting board or other flat surface that has been lightly floured. Knead the dough until smooth and elastic, about 8 minutes.

Lightly oil a large bowl, then put the dough in the bowl, turning it so that the surface of the dough is coated with the oil. Cover the bowl with a damp cloth, and let the dough rise in a warm place for about 1 hour, or until the dough is doubled in volume. Take the dough out of the bowl and place on a lightly floured surface, then divide into two equal pieces. Form into loaves, then place each loaf into a 9" x 5" loaf pan that has been lightly greased. Cover the loaves with a damp cloth, and let rise until doubled in volume, about 45 minutes.

Preheat oven to 350°. Put loaves in oven and bake until the tops are golden brown, about 30 to 45 minutes.

Egg Crescent Rolls

- 6 eggs
- 6 cups flour
- 6 tablespoons sugar
- ½ cup warm water
- 6 tablespoons vegetable oil
- 2 teaspoons salt
- 2 (.25 oz.) packages active dry yeast
- ½ cup butter, softened

Dissolve the yeast in a tablespoon of the water and a tablespoon of sugar. In a large mixing bowl, beat together the eggs, sugar, salt, water, and oil, then add the yeast mixture. Slowly add in the flour and work the dough well. Let the dough rise for an hour or so in a warm place, with a damp cloth covering the bowl. When the dough has doubled in volume, punch it down, recover the bowl, and let it rise for at least another hour.

Preheat the oven to 400°. Take the dough out of the bowl and place it on a flat surface. Roll out the dough, and cut into 3 rounded portions, like a piecrust. Lightly spread the butter on the 3 round pieces, then cut each portion into 6 or 8 wedges. Roll the thinnest part of the wedge toward the largest, forming the crescent, then place on a baking dish that has been greased. Continue rolling the wedges until all the dough is used up. Put the baking trays into the oven for 12 to 15 minutes, or until rolls are golden brown.

Fettuccini Alfredo

- ½ pound fettuccini
- ½ cup butter
- ½ cup heavy cream
- 1 cup grated Parmesan cheese
- 2 to 3 sprigs fresh parsley, chopped
- Salt and pepper to taste

Cook the fettuccini following directions on the package. At the same time, cook the butter, heavy cream, Parmesan, and parsley in a nonstick saucepan, over medium heat. Drain the pasta when ready, and place in serving bowl. Pour the sauce over the pasta, and serve.

Pasta Helen

- 1 pound egg noodles
- ¼ cup olive oil
- 3 cloves garlic, chopped
- 1 cup diced red pepper
- 1 cup diced green pepper
- 1 cup diced yellow pepper
- 3 to 4 sprigs fresh parsley, chopped without stems
- 3 to 4 leaves fresh basil, chopped
- 1 cup sour cream

- ¼ cup grated Romano cheese
- 1 tablespoon chives
- 1 teaspoon salt
- ½ teaspoon black pepper
- 2 tablespoons butter

Cook the noodles according to the directions on package; when finished, drain and set aside. In the meantime, sauté the olive oil, garlic, pepper, parsley, and basil for about 5 minutes, until soft. Add the sour cream, Romano cheese, chives, salt, pepper, and butter to the vegetables, then slowly bring to a boil. Immediately pour sauce over the noodles, blend, and serve.

Fettuccini Pronto

- ½ pound fettuccini
- 2 tablespoons olive oil
- 1 onion, chopped
- 2 cloves garlic, chopped
- 1 red pepper, cut into thin slices
- 1 small hot pepper, sliced
- 1 cup zucchini, sliced
- 2 cups cooked broccoli
- 3 to 4 leaves mint, chopped
- 1 cup sliced mushrooms
- ½ cup black olives
- 3 to 4 sprigs parsley, chopped without stems
- 3 to 4 leaves basil, chopped
- ½ cup dry white wine or water

- ½ cup dry vermouth
- ½ cup heavy cream
- ½ cup grated Parmesan cheese
- ½ cup grated Romano cheese or other hard cheese
- 3 tablespoons pignoli (pine nuts)
- Salt and pepper to taste

The sauce can be prepared in a large sauté pan or in an electric wok set at 325°. Put olive oil in the pan or wok, and heat slightly to allow oil to cover surface of pan. Add onions, garlic, red pepper, hot pepper, zucchini, broccoli, and mint, then sauté together for about 5 minutes. Add the mushrooms, black olives, and wine, then season to taste with salt and pepper, parsley, and basil. Allow to cook on medium heat for 10 minutes.

Cook fettuccini according to the directions on package. Drain the pasta, return to the pot, and add the vegetable mixture to it. Then add the vermouth, heavy cream, cheeses, and pignoli, stirring well to blend. Let rest for a few minutes over a low heat, then serve.

_____

Lasagna

- 1 box lasagna noodles
- 2 pounds whole ricotta
- ½ cup grated Fontinella
- ½ cup grated Asiago
- ½ cup provolone
- 1 cup heavy cream
- 3 eggs

- ½ cup sifted flour
- 8 ounces softened cream cheese
- 1 pound grated mozzarella
- 3 tablespoons olive oil
- 4 sprigs chopped parsley, without stems
- 3 leaves basil, chopped
- 1 teaspoon salt
- ½ teaspoon cinnamon
- 16-ounce jar tomato sauce
- ¼ cup grated Parmesan

Preheat the oven to 350°. Cook the noodles according to the directions on the package. Drain, rinse with cool water, and set aside while you prepare the cheese mixture. Mix together the ricotta, Fontinella, Asiago, provolone, heavy cream, eggs, flour, cream cheese, mozzarella, olive oil, parsley, basil, salt, and cinnamon. Put a thin layer of the sauce into the bottom of a 9" x 13" baking dish, then place a single layer of the noodles on top of the sauce (the noodles can overlap a bit). Divide the cheese mixture roughly in half, then spoon one of the halves over the noodles. Spread carefully with a spatula, covering the noodles. Add a thin layer of sauce over the cheese mixture, then add another single layer of noodles. Cover with the remaining cheese mixture, then the sauce. Add a final single layer of noodles, and the remainder of the sauce. Sprinkle the Parmesan over the top of the lasagna.

Place the baking dish on a baking tray to catch any overspill from the lasagna, then put into the oven. Cook for 1 hour. Let cool for a few minutes, then cut into even pieces and serve.

Linguine with Clam Sauce (Red)

- 1 pound linguine
- 1 tablespoon olive oil
- 1 tablespoon butter
- 2 minced garlic cloves
- 1 small onion, chopped
- 2 stalks celery, chopped
- ½ teaspoon red pepper flakes
- 3 sprigs parsley, chopped
- 1 teaspoon dried oregano
- 3 basil leaves, chopped, or ½ teaspoon dried basil
- 1 teaspoon thyme
- 28-ounce can plum tomatoes, chopped
- ½ cup dry red or white wine
- 2 tablespoons cream sherry
- 2 cans (6.5 ounces each) minced clams, drained

Sauté the olive oil and butter with the minced garlic, onion, celery, red pepper flakes, parsley, oregano, basil, and thyme. Cook for about 5 minutes, then add the plum tomatoes, wine, sherry, and clams. Cook for about thirty minutes. In the meantime, cook the linguine according to the directions on the package; drain and set aside when done. When sauce is done, pour over the linguine and serve with grated Parmesan cheese on the side.

White Sauce

Follow the same steps as above only skip the tomatoes and add instead ½ cup of dry and ½ cup of sweet white wine. To thicken the mixture stir in 2 tablespoons of flour.

Deviled Crab Cakes

- 2 cups lump crabmeat
- 1 egg
- ¼ cup Parmesan or Romano cheese, grated
- ¼ cup olive oil
- 1 tablespoon butter
- 1 small Vidalia onion, finely chopped
- 2 garlic cloves, minced
- 1 red pepper, diced
- ¼ cup fresh parsley, chopped
- ¼ cup chives, chopped
- 2 tablespoons flour
- 1 cup milk
- ⅓ cup Swiss cheese, melted
- ¼ cup mayonnaise
- 1 tablespoon fresh lemon juice
- 1 teaspoon lemon zest
- 1 tablespoon brandy
- A few drops of Tabasco sauce
- A few drops of Worcestershire sauce
- 1 teaspoon red pepper flakes

Sauté the olive oil, butter, onion, garlic, red pepper, parsley, and chives together, about 5 minutes. Stirring constantly, add the flour then slowly pour in the milk, Swiss cheese, and mayonnaise. As this mixture begins to bubble gently, add the lemon juice, lemon zest, brandy, Tabasco, Worcestershire, and red pepper flakes. Simmer.

Preheat the oven to 350°. Beat 1 egg and stir into the sauce until thoroughly blended. Fold in the grated cheese, and if necessary, thicken the sauce with a bit of cornstarch. Add the crabmeat to the sauce and blend thoroughly. Distribute the blended crab mixture into 8 crab cake molds, or shape 8 to 10 cakes and place on a greased baking tray. Refrigerate the crab cakes for at least an hour. Bake approximately 25 minutes.

Cauliflower Casserole

- 1 large head of cauliflower
- ¼ cup butter, melted
- ¼ cup olive oil
- 2 to 3 garlic cloves, chopped
- ½ cup heavy cream
- ½ teaspoon salt
- Seasonal herbs, to taste
- ½ cup cheddar cheese, shredded
- ¼ cup sour cream
- 1 teaspoon Dijon mustard
- Dash of Worcestershire sauce
- ½ cup coarse breadcrumbs
- ¼ cup red pepper, diced

Cook the cauliflower in a large pot for 10 to 15 minutes, then drain and set in a bowl. Break the cauliflower into pieces, then drizzle the butter and olive oil over the cauliflower.

Preheat the oven to 325°. Into a pan set over medium heat, add the heavy cream, salt, and seasonal herbs, then bring to a boil. Add cheddar cheese, sour cream, Dijon mustard, and Worcestershire sauce, blending thoroughly. Turn the heat down to low. Place the cauliflower pieces into a 9" x 13" baking dish, then pour the sauce on top. Top with the breadcrumbs and red pepper, cover the dish with aluminum foil, and place in the oven for 45 minutes.

––––––––––

Baked Zucchini

- 3 to 4 medium-sized zucchini
- 1 onion, chopped
- 1 red pepper, diced
- 1 green pepper, diced
- 1 potato, grated
- 1 cup carrots, shredded
- ½ cup olive oil
- ¼ cup butter, melted
- 1 cup sour cream
- ¼ cup mayonnaise
- ½ cup heavy cream
- 2 to 3 garlic cloves, minced
- 1 teaspoon dried basil, or 3 to 4 leaves, chopped
- 3 sprigs parsley, chopped
- Salt and pepper to taste

- 1 cup breadcrumbs
- 1 cup grated cheese (e.g., cheddar, mozzarella, Swiss)

Preheat the oven to 325°. Grate the unpeeled zucchini into a bowl, and squeeze out the moisture. Add the onion, red and green peppers, potato, and carrots. Mix well, then add the olive oil, butter, sour cream, mayonnaise, heavy cream, basil, parsley, garlic, salt, and pepper. Blend together, then pour mixture into a 9" x 13" baking dish that has been greased and floured. Top casserole with the breadcrumbs and grated cheese, then put into the oven for 1 hour before serving.

Baked Yams

- 4 large yams or sweet potatoes
- 4 carrots, cooked and sliced thick
- 16-ounce can crushed pineapple
- 1 tablespoon orange zest
- 1 tablespoon lemon zest
- Juice of 1 orange
- ¼ cup light corn syrup
- 1 teaspoon cornstarch, diluted with 2 tablespoons water
- ¼ cup sugar
- ½ cup melted butter
- ½ teaspoon salt
- Dash of nutmeg, dried or fresh grated

Boil the yams until they are soft, about 20 minutes. Cool them down enough so you can peel them, then slice into a 9" x 13" baking dish that has been greased. Preheat the oven to 325°. Add the carrots to the yams and mix together gently. Cover the carrots and yams with the pineapple. In a separate bowl, mix together the orange and lemon zest, orange juice, corn syrup, cornstarch, sugar, butter, salt, and nutmeg. Pour the syrup over the yams and carrots, then bake for 30 to 45 minutes, or until the casserole bubbles at the sides of the dish.

Fried Flounder

- 1½ pounds flounder fillets
- 1 egg
- 1 cup flour
- ½ teaspoon baking powder
- ½ teaspoon salt
- ½ teaspoon paprika
- ½ teaspoon black pepper
- 1 teaspoon dried parsley
- 1 cup beer
- 2 cups breadcrumbs
- ½ cup vegetable oil
- 1 lemon, sliced in quarters or rounds
- 2 to 3 sprigs fresh parsley

Set aside the fish and the breadcrumbs, then make the batter by mixing all the other ingredients together. Put the breadcrumbs in a separate dish, and place the dishes side by side. Dip one fillet at a time in the batter, coat thoroughly, then dip into the breadcrumbs. Layer battered fillets on a plate until all are coated.

Heat half of the vegetable oil in a skillet for 1 to 2 minutes over medium heat. Place the fillets in the pan to make one layer. Cook for about 2½ minutes, then gently turn fillets to brown on the other side for another 2½ minutes. When done, use a slotted spatula or flat spoon to transfer to a serving platter. Continue to cook fillets until all are done, then serve with slices of fresh lemon and parsley sprigs on top. Tartar sauce can accompany the fish. (A simple tartar sauce can be made by mixing 1 tablespoon mayonnaise with 2 tablespoons pickle relish.)

Meatballs

- 2 pounds lean ground beef
- 2 cups moistened white bread cubes
- 4 eggs
- ½ cup Romano cheese
- 2 teaspoons salt
- 2 teaspoons pepper
- ¼ cup fresh parsley, chopped
- 3 garlic cloves, minced
- ½ teaspoon fennel seeds
- 1 teaspoon basil, fresh or dried
- 3 tablespoons cream sherry (optional)
- 3 tablespoons olive oil

Put the beef in a large mixing bowl and add the remaining ingredients to the bowl. Blend the mixture with your hands, until everything is combined. Shape the meat mixture into small, round balls and place on a baking dish. Use a spatula to flatten the meatballs a bit. Heat the olive oil in a skillet, then place the meatballs in the pan, leaving space around them to turn the meatballs so that they are browned on all sides. Cook for about 5 minutes total, then transfer to a plate lined with paper towels to drain the oil. When all the meatballs are done, add to a large pan filled with sauce and cook over a medium low heat for about 15 to 20 minutes, or serve the meatballs sprinkled with Parmesan cheese on a platter with sauce on the side. (Another option would be to use the same meat-balls, once cooked, in marinara or tomato sauce to serve with spaghetti or to roll the meatballs small enough to accompany wedding soup.)

Pepper Steak

- 1 pound flank steak
- 4–6 fresh sandwich rolls
- 2 tablespoons olive oil
- 1 red pepper, sliced thin
- 1 green pepper, sliced thin
- 1 small onion, sliced thin
- 2 garlic cloves, sliced
- 1 teaspoon black pepper
- 1 tablespoon Worcestershire sauce
- 1 tablespoon flour
- ½ cup dry red wine
- ½ teaspoon salt

Marinate a flank steak in Italian salad dressing or another marinade of your choice, for 2 hours or more in the refrig-erator. Broil or grill the steak for about 10 minutes, turning halfway through the cooking process. When done, cover with aluminum foil and set aside.

Mix together in a bowl the red and green pepper, onion, garlic, salt, black pepper, and Worcestershire sauce. Heat the olive oil in a skillet over a medium heat, then sauté the pepper mix for about 5 minutes, until soft. Add the flour and red wine, blending together. Cook a few more minutes until the mixture thickens a bit. Slice the steak, place several pieces on a bun, pour some of the pepper mix over the beef, and serve.

Chicken Cacciatore

- 3 pounds chicken pieces
- 1 cup flour
- 1 cup cornstarch
- 1 teaspoon each seasoning of your choice (e.g., oregano, sage, rosemary, thyme)
- 1 teaspoon salt
- 1 teaspoon black pepper
- ½ cup vegetable or sesame oil
- 1 onion, sliced thin
- 2 garlic cloves, crushed
- 1 cup mushrooms
- ½ cup yellow pepper, diced
- 4 leaves basil, chopped
- 4 sprigs parsley, chopped
- 16-ounce can crushed tomatoes, drained
- ½ cup red wine
- 1 teaspoon oregano
- 1 tablespoon flour

Put the flour, cornstarch, seasonings, salt, and pepper into a one-gallon freezer bag. Add the chicken pieces to the bag, one or two at a time, coat thoroughly, then put on a plate. When all the pieces are coated, heat the oil in a large skillet over medium heat, and add the chicken pieces to the pan in a single layer. Cook on one side for about 5 minutes, then turn and cook on the other side for 5 minutes. Remove the pieces from the pan, and set aside. Finish cooking the rest of the chicken in this manner. When all the chicken has been browned, add the onion, garlic, mushrooms, yellow pepper, basil, and parsley to the skillet. Sauté for about 5 minutes, adding a little more oil if needed. When the vegetables are soft, add the tomatoes, wine, and oregano, bringing to a simmer. Stir in a tablespoon of flour to thicken the mixture, if needed.

Preheat the oven to 350°. Arrange the chicken pieces in a large baking dish, then pour the vegetable mixture over the pieces. Spread the grated cheese over the top of the casserole, and heat in the oven for 15 to 20 minutes.

Veal Scaloppini

- 1 pound veal scaloppini, or cutlets pounded thin
- 2 eggs
- ½ cup heavy cream
- 5 sprigs parsley, chopped
- ½ cup Parmesan cheese, grated
- 1 cup breadcrumbs
- 3 tablespoons vegetable or olive oil
- ¼ pound sliced prosciutto

- ¼ pound provolone, sliced thin
- 1 cup beef bouillon
- 2 tablespoons red wine
- ½ pound sliced mushrooms
- 1 tablespoon cornstarch, diluted with 1 tablespoon beef bouillon
- Salt and pepper to taste

Beat the eggs together in a shallow bowl. Add the heavy cream, half of the chopped parsley, salt, black pepper, and Parmesan cheese. Put the breadcrumbs in a separate bowl, next to the egg batter. Dip the veal, one piece at a time, into the egg batter, then into the breadcrumbs, making sure each piece is thoroughly coated. Heat the oil in a large skillet over medium heat, then brown the veal in a single layer, 2 to 3 minutes on each side. Continue cooking until all the veal is cooked, then set aside and cover with aluminum foil.

In a separate pan, bring the bouillon to a boil, then add the red wine, remaining parsley, mushrooms, and cornstarch. Cook for about 5 minutes over a medium-low heat. Transfer the veal to an ovenproof platter or shallow baking dish, large enough to arrange the meat in a single layer. Place a slice of prosciutto and a slice of provolone on each piece of veal, then pour the sauce over the veal. Place the platter under the broiler for about 3 minutes, until the cheese has melted.

Piecrust

- 3 cups sifted flour
- ½ teaspoon salt
- 1 cup Crisco shortening
- ½ cup ice water

Use a pastry cutter to mix the flour, salt, and shortening together. Mixture will be thick and crumbly. Add half the water, slowly, and continue mixing until dough starts to form. Add more of the water as needed, until dough comes together in a ball. To make the dough easier to roll, wrap in plastic and place in the refrigerator for 30 minutes.

Preheat oven to 425°. Place the dough on a floured surface. Using a rolling pin, press down on the dough and roll into a rough circle, wide enough on all sides to fit into a pie dish and hang over the sides. When dough is rolled out, place into pie dish. Bring edges in to form a fluted crust by going around the dish and pressing edge together with your fingers. Before baking, use a fork to prick the bottom of the crust to keep it from rising. Bake for 10 to 12 minutes, or until edges and bottom are golden brown. Remove from oven and cool.

Lemon Meringue Pie

- ½ cup sugar
- 3 egg yolks, beaten; set aside the whites for the meringue
- 1½ cups water
- ½ cup fresh lemon juice
- 3 tablespoons cornstarch
- 6 tablespoons sugar
- ½ teaspoon salt
- 2 teaspoons lemon zest
- 1 tablespoon butter
- ½ teaspoon vanilla
- ¼ teaspoon cream of tartar
- 1 to 2 drops of yellow food coloring (optional)

In a saucepan, mix together the sugar, cornstarch, and salt. Add in the egg yolks, water, lemon juice, lemon zest, butter, and food coloring. Cook slowly over a low heat, stirring constantly, until mixture thickens into a custard. Cool, then pour into the baked piecrust.

Preheat the oven to 350°. In a separate bowl, beat the egg whites and cream of tartar until the egg whites are thick and foamy. Add the sugar, one tablespoon at a time, and then the vanilla. Beat until the egg whites form stiff peaks. Spoon meringue onto top of lemon custard, and bake until the meringue turns light brown, about 10 minutes. Let the pie cool away from drafts, so the meringue does not droop.

Fast Scratch Cake

- 2 cups sifted flour
- 2 eggs
- ½ cup sugar
- ½ cup corn syrup
- ½ cup vegetable oil
- ¼ cup milk
- ¼ cup orange juice
- 3 teaspoons baking powder
- 1 teaspoon salt
- 1 teaspoon vanilla
- 1 teaspoon orange extract
- 1 tablespoon orange zest

Preheat the oven to 325°. Mix together the flour, salt, sugar, and baking powder. In a separate bowl, lightly beat together the corn syrup, milk, vegetable oil, eggs, vanilla, orange extract, orange juice, and zest. Add liquid to the flour mixture and blend together, adding a bit more flour if needed to make a smooth batter. Pour into a greased and floured Bundt pan, then bake for about 1 hour. Cool the cake for about 10 minutes, then remove from pan onto a round serving dish.

Make a glaze for the cake by heating 3 tablespoons of orange juice in a small saucepan with ¼ cup powdered sugar, until thickened slightly, about 5 minutes. Let cool for a bit, then use a fork to prick some holes in the top of the cake. Drizzle the glaze over the top and serve.

Anisette Cookies

- 4 eggs
- 1 cup vegetable oil
- ½ cup anisette liqueur
- ½ cup milk
- 4 teaspoons anise extract
- 1½ cups sugar
- 5 cups sifted flour
- 5 teaspoons baking powder
- Extra flour for rolling cookies

Mix eggs, oil, and anisette liqueur. Add the milk and anise extract, then beat the ingredients well. Add sugar, flour, and baking powder, then mix into a dough.

Preheat oven to 350°. The dough will be sticky, so put some flour on your hands to roll the dough into small balls, about 1 inch in diameter. Bake on a lightly greased and floured baking sheet for about 15 minutes. Remove from oven. Make an icing by heating 1 cup powdered sugar in a small saucepan with ¼ cup milk and 1 tablespoon anisette liqueur. Transfer to a bowl and dip the cookies in the icing, then set on a plate to cool.

Tomato Sauce with Meat

- ½ pound ground round steak
- Two 28-ounce cans tomato puree
- 8-ounce can tomato paste
- 8 ounces tomato juice
- 1 pound ground pork
- 3 garlic cloves, sliced thin
- 1 onion, chopped (or 2 shallots, chopped)
- 6 leaves fresh basil, chopped, or 2 teaspoons dried
- 6 sprigs parsley, chopped
- ½ cup olive oil
- 1 teaspoon fennel seed
- ½ cup red wine
- ½ cup grated Parmesan cheese
- ½ cup grated Romano cheese
- Salt and pepper to taste
- 1 teaspoon red pepper flakes (optional)

In a large cooking pot, heat the olive oil and sauté the garlic and onion (or shallots), for 3 minutes. Add the ground beef and pork, and cook until browned all around. Add the pureed tomatoes, the tomato paste, and the juice, and mix together with the meat. Stir in the basil, parsley, salt, pepper, fennel, and red pepper flakes. Blend everything together, and bring to a boil. Lower heat, and add the wine and cheeses. Simmer for 1 hour, uncovered, stirring occasionally. Serve over pasta.

Barbeque Sauce

- 28-ounce can crushed tomatoes
- 8-ounce can tomato paste
- 2 cups diced onions
- ½ cup vegetable broth
- 1 tablespoon brown sugar
- 5 cloves garlic, crushed
- ½ cup cider vinegar
- ½ cup honey
- 1 tablespoon Tabasco sauce
- 1 jalapeno pepper, diced and seeded (you may need to wear thin plastic gloves to do this, so the pepper does not burn your fingers)
- 2 tablespoons "liquid smoke" flavoring
- Salt and pepper to taste

In a large saucepan, mix together the vegetable broth and brown sugar. Heat slowly, then add the onions and allow them to caramelize, about 10 minutes. Add the tomatoes and garlic, and bring to a boil over medium heat, stirring constantly. Lower the heat to simmer, and add the cider vinegar. Add salt and pepper to taste.

Simmer the sauce prepared so far for 1 hour, then add the honey, Tabasco sauce, jalapeño pepper, and tomato paste. Cover the pot and simmer the sauce for 40 to 50 minutes. Remove the lid and add the liquid smoke. Taste a spoonful of the sauce, let cool for a few seconds, then taste it and see if you need any more salt or pepper. Use as needed on chicken, pork, or ribs.

Three - Bean Chili

- 2 large center-cut pork chops
- 8-ounce can chickpeas (garbanzo beans), drained
- 8-ounce can red kidney beans, drained
- 8-ounce can black beans, drained
- Two 8-ounce cans tomato sauce
- 4 tablespoons olive oil, plus extra for the pork
- 5 carrots, peeled and chopped
- 2 stalks celery, chopped
- 3 cloves garlic, minced
- 1 medium red onion, diced
- 1 green pepper, diced
- 1 red pepper, diced
- 1 teaspoon dried parsley
- 2 teaspoons fennel seeds
- 2 teaspoons fajita seasoning
- ¼ cup ketchup
- ¼ cup cream sherry
- ½ teaspoon cayenne pepper

Coat the pork chops lightly with olive oil. Season them with salt and pepper, and a teaspoon of fennel seeds, then roast in a 350° oven for about 25 minutes until they are almost cooked. Cool, then cut into cubes and set aside.

In a large sauce pot, heat 2 tablespoons olive oil over medium heat, then sauté the garlic, red onion, celery, carrots, and red and green peppers for about 7 minutes. Add the chickpeas, kidney beans, and black beans to the vegetables, mixing well.

Add the tomato sauce, ketchup, and cream sherry to the saucepan, along with the cayenne pepper, parsley flakes, fennel seeds, and fajita seasoning. Bring to a low boil, then add the pork and lower the heat to medium low. Cook for 1 hour, occasionally stirring the chili.

Notes

1. Quoted in Ronda de Sola Chervin, *Quotable Saints* (Oak Lawn, Ill.: CMJ Marian, 1992), p. 164.
2. See *The Rule of St. Benedict*, ed. Thomas Fry (Collegeville, Minn.: Liturgical, 1981).
3. St. Thomas Aquinas, quoted in Jill Haak Adels, ed., *The Wisdom of the Saints: An Anthology* (New York: Oxford University Press, 1989), p. 168.
4. Quoted in Ronda De Sola Chervin, *Quotable Saints*, p. 120.
5. Quoted in *The Country Parson, The Temple* in The Classics of Western Spirituality, ed. John N. Wall (New York: Paulist, 1981), p. 316. Used with permission.
6. See Guigo II, *The Ladder of Monks and Twelve Meditations*, trans. Edmund Colledge and James Walsh (Kalamazoo, Mich.: Cistercian, 1981), pp. 67–86.
7. Richard A. Swenson, *More Than Meets the Eye: Fascinating Glimpses of God's Power and Design* (Colorado Springs: NavPress, 2000), pp. 85–86.
8. Swenson, pp. 85–86.
9. Swenson, p. 87.
10. Swenson, p. 97.

Recommended Reading

Guigo II. *The Ladder of Monks and Twelve Meditations,* trans. Edmund Colledge and James Walsh. Kalamazoo, Mich.: Cistercian, 1981.

Herbert, George. *The Country Parson, The Temple* in The Classics of Western Spirituality, ed. John N. Wall. New York: Paulist, 1981.

Muto, Susan. *One in the Lord: Living Our Call to Christian Community.* Hyde Park, N.Y.: New City, 2013.

Ryken, Leland, et al., eds. *Dictionary of Biblical Imagery.* Downers Grove, Ill.: InterVarsity, 1998.

Stone, Rachel Marie. *Eat with Joy: Redeeming God's Gift of Food.* Downers Grove, Ill.: InterVarsity, 2013.

Swenson, Richard A. *More than Meets the Eye: Fascinating Glimpses of God's Power and Design.* Colorado Springs: NavPress, 2000.

Yancey, Philip and Paul Brand. *Fearfully and Wonderfully Made.* Grand Rapids: Zondervan, 1987.

ABOUT THE AUTHOR

Susan Muto is the executive director of the Epiphany Association, a nonprofit ecumenical education, consultation, and research center. A prolific author and internationally renowned teacher and speaker, she holds an M.A. and PH.D. in English literature from the University of Pittsburgh.